Herbert A. Grueber

Roman Medallions in the British Museum

Herbert A. Grueber

Roman Medallions in the British Museum

ISBN/EAN: 9783743322240

Manufactured in Europe, USA, Canada, Australia, Japa

Cover: Foto ©ninafisch / pixelio.de

Manufactured and distributed by brebook publishing software (www.brebook.com)

Herbert A. Grueber

Roman Medallions in the British Museum

CATALOGUE

OF THE

ROMAN COINS

IN THE

BRITISH MUSEUM.

LONDON:
PRINTED BY ORDER OF THE TRUSTEES.

LONGMANS & CO., PATERNOSTER ROW; B. M. PICKERING, 196, PICCADILLY;
B. QUARITCH, 15, PICCADILLY; AND
A. ASHER & CO., 13, BEDFORD STREET, COVENT GARDEN, AND AT BERLIN.

PARIS: MM. C. ROLLIN & FEUARDENT, 4, PLACE LOUVOIS.

ROMAN MEDALLIONS

IN THE

BRITISH MUSEUM.

BY

HERBERT A. GRUEBER.

EDITED BY

REGINALD STUART POOLE.

LONDON:
PRINTED BY ORDER OF THE TRUSTEES.
1874.

PREFACE.

This volume contains a Catalogue of the Roman Medallions in the British Museum. The metal of each specimen is given, and its size in inches and tenths. The weight of all examples in gold and silver is stated in English grains. Tables for converting grains into grammes, and inches into millimètres, as well as into the measures of Mionnet's scale, are given at the end of the volume (pp. 152–154). A table of dates and titles also there given (pp. 131–151) will enable the reader to find the year or period to which each medallion may be ascribed.

Every medallion of interest is figured in the plates, which are executed by the Autotype mechanical process from casts in plaster, except in the case of the finest specimens, which are from drawings by Miss Godsall.

The work has been drawn up under my direction by Mr. Herbert A. Grueber, Assistant in the Department of Coins and Medals. In the revision I have had the valuable aid of Mr. Head, Assistant Keeper, and Mr. Gardner, Assistant in the same Department.

REGINALD STUART POOLE.

CONTENTS.

	PAGE
Domitian	1
Trajan	2
Hadrian	3
Aelius Caesar	6
Antoninus Pius	7
Faustina the Elder	12
Marcus Aurelius	13
Marcus Aurelius and Commodus	15
Faustina the Younger	16
Lucius Verus	18
Lucilla	19
Commodus and Annius Verus	20
Commodus	21
Commodus and Crispina	31
Septimius Severus	32
Julia Domna	34
Caracalla	35
Geta	36
Elagabalus	37
Severus Alexander	38
Severus Alexander and Julia Mamaea	41
Julia Mamaea	42
Maximin I.	43
Pupienus	44
Gordian III.	45
Philip I.	50
Otacilia	51
Philip I. and Philip II.	52
Philip I., Otacilia, and Philip II.	53
Otacilia, Philip I., and Philip II.	55
Philip II.	56
Gallus	57
Gallus and Volusian	59
Volusian	60

CONTENTS.

	PAGE
Valerian	61
Valerian, Valerian the Younger, Gallienus, and Salonina	62
Valerian and Gallienus	63
Gallienus	64
Gallienus and Salonina	67
Gallienus and Saloninus	68
Salonina	69
Saloninus	70
Claudius II. (Gothicus)	71
Tacitus	72
Florianus	73
Probus	74
Carus	76
Numerian	77
Carinus	78
Diocletian	79
Maximian I.	81
Constantius I. (Chlorus)	82
Helena	83
Galerius	84
Constantine I. (The Great)	85
Constantine II.	87
Constans	88
Constantius II.	90
Magnentius	93
Decentius	94
Constantius Gallus	95
Julian II.	96
Valentinian I.	97
Valens	98
Gratian	99
Honorius	100
Attalus	101
INDEXES:—	
I. Names	103
II. Reverse-Inscriptions	107
III. Mints	115
IV. Types	117
Table of Dates and Titles	131
Table of the relative Weights of English Grains and French Grammes	152
Table for converting English Inches into Millimètres and the measures of Mionnet's Scale	154

DOMITIAN.

(DOMITIANVS GERMANICVS.)

CAES. A.D. 69: AUG. A.D. 81: DIED A.D. 96.

1. Obv. IMP·CAES·DOMIT·AVG·GERM·P·M·TR·POT·V· Head of Domitian r., laur.: border of dots.

   Rev. IMP VIII·COS·XI CENS POT·P·P Germania, with dishevelled hair, wearing braccae and cloak over r. knee, seated r. in an attitude of grief on an ornamented oblong shield; her r. hand rests on the shield, and her l. supports her head; below the shield, a broken spear: border of dots.   Æ 1·3. Wt. 264·1 grs. Pl. I. fig. 1.

2. Obv. IMP·CAES·DOMIT·AVG· GERM P·M·TR·POT V Bust of Domitian r., laur., wearing aegis: border of dots.

   Rev. IMP VIII COS XI· CENS POT PP Minerva, helmeted, and wearing tunic, aegis, and peplum, seated l. on throne, her feet on footstool; she holds on r. hand Victory l. with wreath and palm, and with l. hand sceptre; her l. arm rests upon a round shield, on which are represented two temples, and below them four small figures; the shield is supported on the head of a captive, seated l. on prow l.: border of dots.   Æ 1·35. Wt. 402·5 grs. Pl. I. fig. 2.

3. Obv. IMP CAES DOMIT AVG GERM PM TR P XI Head of Domitian r., laur.: border of dots.

   Rev. IMP·XXI·COS·XVI·CENS·PPP Minerva standing l. on summit of rostral column, helmeted, wearing doubled tunic and aegis; the aegis covers her breast, hangs down behind as far as her knees, and has a fringe of serpents; she bears shield on l. arm, and hurls spear with r. hand; at her feet, owl r.; the shaft of the column is ornamented with figures: border of dots.   Æ 1·15. Wt. 270·2 grs.

4. Obv. IMP CAES DIVI VESP F DOMIT AVG GERM COS XI Bust of Domitian r., laur., wearing aegis: border of dots.

   Rev. No inscription. Similar type and same border as no. 2.   Æ 1·4.

TRAJAN.

(NERVA TRAIANVS OPTIMVS GERMANICVS DACICVS PARTHICVS.)

Caes. a.d. 97: Aug. a.d. 98: Died a.d. 117.

1. Obv. **IMP CAES NERVAE TRAIANO AVG GER DAC PM TR P COS V P P** Bust of Trajan r., laur., wearing ægis.

    Rev. **ADVENTVS AVG** (In exergue) **SPQR OPT PRINCIPI** Emperor, wearing paludamentum and cuirass, and holding spear, on horseback r.; he is preceded by Felicitas, clad in tunic and peplum, and carrying caduceus and cornucopiæ, and is followed by three prætorian soldiers, the nearest armed with spear and shield.
    $\mathcal{R}$ 1·3. Wt. 319·6 grs. Pl. I. fig. 3.

2. Obv. **IMP[CAES NER]VAE TRAIANO AVG GER DAC PM TR PCOS PP** Bust of Trajan l., laur., wearing paludamentum and cuirass.

    Rev. **VRBS RO M A AETERNA** Emperor r., wearing pontifical robes and holding patera, **sacrificing at a** garlanded and lighted altar, placed in front of a **hexastylo** temple of the Corinthian order; behind him, two attendants, one of whom appears to be an ædituus; on r. of altar, a camillus, facing, holding acerra; behind him, an attendant, and on his l., a victimarius with bull; between the altar and the temple, a tibicen, facing, playing double flute: the tympanum of the pediment of the temple is ornamented with a standing figure between two others recumbent; on each angle of the pediment is a trophy, and on the apex, a seated figure between two Victories. Æ 1·4.

3. Obv. **IMP CAES NERVA TRAIAN AVG GERM DACICVS PM** Bust of Trajan r., laur., wearing paludamentum.

    Rev. **TR P VII IMP IIII COS V PP** Emperor, holding laurel-branch in r. hand, in triumphal quadriga r.; horses walking; the chariot is ornamented with reliefs. Æ 1·3.

HADRIAN.

(TRAIANVS HADRIANVS OPTIMVS, GERMANICVS, DACICVS, PARTHICVS.)

Aug. a.d. 117: Died a.d. 138.

1. Obv. **IMP CAESAR TRAIA NVS HADRIANVS AVG** Bust of Hadrian l., laur., wearing paludamentum and cuirass.
   Rev. **PONT M A X TR POT COS III** Felicitas l., wearing stephane, tunic, and peplum; she holds winged caduceus with r. hand and cornucopiæ with l.: border of dots.
   Æ 1·4. Wt. 330·8 grs. Pl. II. fig. 1.

2. Obv. **IMP CAESAR TRAI ANVS·HADRIANVS AVG** Bust of Hadrian l., laur.: border of dots.
   Rev. **PONT MAX TR POT COS III** Jupiter, wearing pallium which hangs from l. shoulder and covers his knees, seated l., his feet on footstool; on r. hand he holds Victory l. with wreath and palm, and with l. hand sceptre: border of dots. Æ 1·45. Wt. 395·4 grs. Pl. II. fig. 2.

3. Obv. **HADRIANVS AVG COS III PP** Bust of Hadrian l., bareheaded, wearing paludamentum and cuirass: border of dots.
   Rev. **ANNO NA AVGVSTI CERES** (In exergue) **COS III PP** Ceres, wearing tunic and peplum veiling the head which is wreathed with corn; she is seated l., on cista, her feet on footstool, and holds ears of corn and lighted torch; around the cista a serpent entwines itself; before her, Annona, standing r., wearing tunic and peplum, resting r. hand on her hip and holding cornucopiæ with l.; between them, an altar, on which is placed a modius; in the background, a prow r.: border of dots. Æ 1·5. Pl. II. fig. 3.

4. Obv. **HADRIANVS AVG COS III PP** Head of Hadrian r., bare: border of dots.
   Rev. **CON COR DIA** (In exergue) **COS II** Emperor and Ælius Cæsar, both togate, standing face to face and grasping r. hands; between them, Concordia, facing, wearing tunic and peplum, resting a hand on the shoulder of each: border of dots. Æ 1·5. Pl. III. fig. 1.

5. Obv. **HADRIANVS AVGVSTVS** Bust of Hadrian r., laur., wearing paludamentum: border of dots.
   Rev. **COS III** Hercules r., resting r. hand on club, and holding with l. branch of apple-tree, over shoulder; on l. arm hangs the lion's skin: border of dots. Æ 1·4. Pl. III. fig. 2.

6. Obv. HADRIANVS AVGVSTVS PP Bust of Hadrian r., laur., wearing paludamentum and cuirass: border of dots.
   Rev. COS III (in exergue) Salus r., wearing peplum, and resting l. hand on shoulder of young Æsculapius, facing, wearing wreath and chlamys which hangs down from l. shoulder over arm; he rests l. hand on his hip, and holds with r. staff, around which serpent entwines itself, and feeds from r. hand of Salus; on r., a column, surmounted by figure of Apollo, holding bow? border of dots. Æ 1·45.

7. Obv. Same inscription. Head of Hadrian r., radiate: border of dots.
   Rev. Same. Æ 1·1. Pl. III. fig. 3.

8. Obv. HADRIANVS AVGVSTVS Bust of Hadrian r., laur., wearing paludamentum: border of dots.
   Rev. COS III Eagle l., looking back, on thunderbolt, between, on the right, peacock, displayed l., on sceptre, and, on the left, owl r., on convex shield ornamented with radiating lines: border of dots.
   Æ 1·35. Pl. IV. fig. 1.

9. Obv. Same inscription. Bust of Hadrian l., bareheaded, wearing paludamentum: border of dots.
   Rev. COS III PP (in exergue) Emperor, wearing paludamentum and cuirass, standing l. between three signa on his r., and an aquila and a signum on his l.; he raises his r. hand and holds spear with l.: border of dots. Æ 1·35. Pl. IV. fig. 2.

10. Obv. HADRIANVS AVG COS III PP Similar type r.: border of dots.
    Rev. COS III PP (in exergue) Emperor, wearing paludamentum and cuirass, on horse galloping l.; he hurls, with r. hand, a javelin at a wild boar before him, already speared: border of dots. Æ 1·3. Pl. IV. fig. 3.

11. Obv. IMP CAESAR HADRIANVS AVG COS III PP Bust of Hadrian r., laur., wearing ægis: border of dots.
    Rev. COS III PP Silvanus, bearded, a chlamys thrown over l. shoulder, walking r., carrying pedum in l. hand, and with r. dragging a ram behind him by the fore-legs; before him, a temple of the Ionic order, of which only one column and a portion of the pediment are seen, and in front of which are seen a lighted altar, and a hen l.; behind Silvanus, a tree: border of dots. Æ 1·15. Pl. V. fig. 1.

12. Obv. HADRIANVS AVG COS III PP Head of Hadrian r., laur.: border of dots.
    Rev. Same. Æ 1·35.

13. Obv. Same inscription. Bust of Hadrian r., bareheaded, wearing paludamentum: border of dots.

Rev. **VENERI GENETRICI** Venus l., wearing stephane, tunic, and **peplum**; she holds on r. hand Victory l., with wreath and **palm, and rests l. on round** shield ornamented with figure of Æneas r., carrying Anchises and leading Iulus; beneath shield, cuirass and helmet: border of dots. Æ 2·15.

    This medallion has a broad rim.

14. Obv. Same inscription. Head of Hadrian l., laur.: border of dots.

Rev. Apollo Citharœdus, with pallium covering his legs, seated r. on rock, playing lyre; before him are three of the Muses standing l.; the centre one, (Polyhymnia,) of shorter stature than the others, leans on column: border of dots. Æ 1·55. Pl. V. fig. 2.

15. Obv. Same inscription. Bust of Hadrian l., bareheaded, wearing paludamentum: border of dots.

Rev. Æsculapius, facing, wearing pallium and leaning on staff, which is placed under his arm and around which serpent entwines itself: border of dots. Æ 2·2. Pl. VI.

    This medallion has a broad rim.

16. Obv. **IMP CAESAR HADRI ANVS AVG COS II PP** Head of Hadrian r., laur.: plain border.

Rev. Emperor on horse cantering r., a little in advance of another horseman armed with spear; before the Emperor, a foot-soldier carrying spear. Æ 1·5.

    This medallion has been tooled and the inscription on the obverse altered: it is described by Cohen in his Monnaies Impériales, vol. II. p. 70, no. 565, as **COSIIIPP**: see also his remarks on the letters **P.P.** at p. 99 of the same volume.

17. Obv. **HADRIANVS** [**AVGVSTVS**] Head of Hadrian, as Hercules, r., wearing lion's skin.

Rev. **TE LLVS** (In exergue) [**S**]**TA**[**BIL**] Tellus reclining l., resting l. arm on a basket, and holding with l. hand a long vine-branch and the end of her peplum which covers her legs; her r. hand is placed upon a globe, around which are the four Seasons, represented as children, with attributes. Æ 1·25.

    For the attributes of the Seasons see no. **22** of the Medallions of Antoninus Pius p. 10.

18. Obv. **HADRIANVS AVGVSTVS P P** Bust of Hadrian r., laur., wearing paludamentum and cuirass: border of dots.

Rev. **VIRTVTI AVGVSTI** Emperor, wearing paludamentum, on horse galloping r.; he **hurls**, with r. hand, javelin **at lion running** before him: border of dots. Æ 1·6.

19. Obv. **HADRIANVS AVGVSTVS** Head of Hadrian r., laur.: border of dots.

Rev. Neptuno r., resting l. **foot on a** rock, and leaning l. elbow on knee, over which hangs **his chlamys**; he holds trident with r. hand; before him, Minerva l., helmeted and wearing doubled tunic, touching with r. hand a branch of an olive-tree, which is between them, and at the foot of which are two serpents; behind Minerva, a shield ornamented with serpent. Æ 1·6.

This medallion has a rim.

AELIUS CAESAR.

(LVCIVS AELIVS CAESAR.)

Caes. a.d. 136: Died a.d. 138.

Obv. **L·AELIVS CAESAR** Bust of Ælius l., bearded, head bare, wearing paludamentum and cuirass: border of dots.

Rev. **CON COR DIA** (In exergue) **COS II** Ælius and Hadrian, both togate, standing face to face and grasping r. hands; between them, Concordia, facing, wearing tunic and peplum, resting a hand on the shoulder of each: border of dots. Æ 1·6. Pl. VII. fig. 1.

ANTONINUS PIUS.

(TITVS AELIVS HADRIANVS ANTONINVS PIVS.)

CAES. A.D. 138: AUG. A.D. 138: DIED A.D. 161.

1. Obv. **IMPT AEL CAES HADRIAN TONINVS AVG PIVS** Bust of Antoninus Pius l., laur., wearing paludamentum: border of dots.

    Rev. **PONT MAX** (In exergue) **TR POT COS II** The Emperor on horseback, or equestrian statue of the Emperor, r., with r. hand raised; he wears paludamentum and cuirass, and has a parazonium slung to his side; the horse is walking: border of dots. Æ 1·5. Pl. VII. fig. 2.

2. Obv. **IMPT AEL CAES HADR ANTONINVS AVG PIVS** Bust of Antoninus Pius r., laur., wearing paludamentum and cuirass: border of dots.

    Rev. **TR POT COS II P P** Apollo Citharœdus, wearing sleeved tunic and peplum, advancing r., holding with l. hand lyre and with r. plectrum; before him, a garlanded altar, on which rests a laurel-branch, and behind him, a tripod with three handles and pendent fillets: border of dots. Æ 1·6. Pl. VIII. fig. 1.

3. Obv. Same.

    Rev. **PM·TR·POT** (beneath) **Victory, in biga r.,** holding **reins with r.**
    COS·II
    hand and **palm with l.**; horses galloping: border of dots.
    Æ 1·55. Pl. VIII. fig. 2.

4. Obv. **ANTONINVS AVG PIVS P P TR P COS III** Head of Antoninus Pius l., laur.: border of dots.

    Rev. **AESCVLAPIVS** (beneath) Galley r., passing beneath a bridge of which two arches are seen; at the stern, a figure with arms extended, and at the prow, a serpent coiled r.; before the galley, Tiber, reclining l., amidst the waters, holding **reed with l. hand** and stretching out r. to welcome the arrival of the serpent; in the background, **an island** on which are walls and gates and a **tree**: border of dots. Æ 1·45. Pl. VIII. fig. 3.

5. Obv. Same inscription. Bust of Antoninus Pius r., laur., wearing paludamentum **and cuirass**: border of dots.

    Rev. Same inscription and border **and similar** type. **Tiber rests l.** arm on urn from which water flows. Æ 1·5.

6. Obv. Same.

Rev. Victory l., wearing long doubled tunic and peplum, holding with l. hand palm and with r. inscribing a shield, which forms part of a trophy; before the trophy, a female figure, in barbarian costume, facing, her hands clasped; she looks at a youth on her r., who raises his l. hand and holds uncertain object with r. : border of dots.

Æ 1·45. Pl. VIII. fig. 4.

7. Obv. ANTONINVS AVG PIVS P P TR P COS IIII Bust of Antoninus Pius r., laur., wearing cuirass : border of dots.

Rev. Sol, radiate, wearing chlamys one end of which is wrapped round his l. arm, holding whip with r. hand and reins with l., stepping into quadriga r., which rises upon the clouds and is preceded by Lucifer bearing torch; horses galloping; beneath the clouds, Tellus, reclining l., with peplum covering her legs, holding ears of corn and cornucopiæ; at her breast, a babe : border of dots. Æ 1·45. Pl. IX. fig. 1.

8. Obv. ANTONINVS AVG PIVS P P TR P COS III . IMP II Head of Antoninus Pius r., laur. : border of dots.

Rev. Youth, standing towards l., wearing cinctus; he holds pedum with l. hand and uncertain object (twisted net ?) with r. : border of dots.

Æ 1·25. Pl. IX. fig. 2.

9. Obv. ANTONINVS AVG · PIVS P P · TR P · Same type and border.

Rev. COS IIII (in exergue) Diana Venatrix, wearing short doubled tunic which leaves r. breast bare, and chlamys tied round waist, running r.; in her extended l. hand she holds bow and arrow, and with r. is drawing an arrow from her quiver, which is slung behind her shoulders; at her feet, a hound running r., and behind her, a tree : border of dots. Æ 1·3. Pl. IX. fig. 3.

10. Obv. ANTONINVS AVG PI VS P P TR P COS IIII Same type and border.

Rev. Diana Lucifera, wearing tunic, seated sideways on horned and winged panther, running l.; she holds bow with r. hand and long lighted torch with l.; her quiver is slung behind her shoulders : border of dots. Æ 1·6. Pl. X. fig. 1.

11. Obv. ANTONINVS AVG PIVS P P TR P COS IIII Same type and border.

Rev. Goddess, wearing stephane and long doubled tunic, standing r.; she holds spear with r. hand and small animal (fawn or capricorn ?) on l. : border of dots. Æ 1·5. Pl. X. fig. 2.

12. Obv. ANTONINVS AVG PIVS P P TR P COS IIII   Bust of Antoninus Pius r., laur., wearing ægis : **border of dots.**

Rev. Minerva r., helmeted, wearing tunic and peplum, holding spear **with** l. hand, and resting **r.** on shield ornamented with serpent; before her, Neptune seated l., his feet on footstool, wearing pallium and holding trident; between them a table, on which is placed a **vase**; behind **the table** a female figure standing **under** an arch, and putting her **r. hand into the vase**: border of dots.   Æ 1·55.   Pl. X. fig. 3.

13. Obv. **Same inscription.**   Head of Antoninus Pius r., laur. : border of dots.

Rev. Roma, helmeted, wearing doubled tunic which leaves r. breast bare, and peplum, seated l., on cuirass; at her side shield, on which are represented the Wolf and Twins; she holds cornucopiæ with l. hand, and with r. presents olive-branch to the Emperor, standing before her togate; between them, in the background, Felicitas l., veiled, resting l. arm on the shoulder of Roma, and holding winged caduceus with r. hand; the Emperor is **accompanied** by Marcus Aurelius, togate, who stands behind him : **border of dots.**   Æ 1·45.   Pl. XI. fig. 1

14. Obv. Same.

Rev. Tellus, **her head bound with wreath, wearing tunic and** peplum, reclining r., her r. arm on **the back of a cow** lying **down** behind **her to** l.; **with r. hand she holds the end** of her peplum, **and with** l. **cornucopiæ which rests on her knee**; she is surrounded **by the four Seasons,** represented as children, **all** of whom are naked, **with the** exception of Winter r. looking back, **who,** hooded and wearing **short tunic**, is seated at her feet, and holds **falx and dried fruits;** Spring stands r., on her l. knee, with **thyrsus in** l. hand; on her lap is Summer, with sickle in l.; and **behind** her, Autumn l., holding patera of fruit ? in **r.**; above, a zone, upon which are **seen the following** signs of the zodiac, Aries, Taurus, Gemini, Cancer, and Leo.

Æ 1·4.   Pl. XI. fig. 2.

15. Obv. **ANTONINVS** AVG PIVS P P TR P COS IIII   Bust of Antoninus Pius l., laur., wearing ægis : border of dots.

Rev. Victory r., wearing peplum, sacrificing bull, which has fallen on the r. fore-leg; she rests her l. knee on his back, and seizing him by the nostrils with her l. hand, is about to strike him with a knife, which **she** holds in her **r.** : border of dots.   Æ 1·5.   Pl. XI. fig. 3.

16. Obv. ANTONINVS AVG PIVS P P TR P XVI   Bust of Antoninus Pius r., bare-headed, wearing ægis : border of dots.

Rev. **COS IIII (in exergue)**   Emperor, togate, seated l. on curule chair, his feet **on footstool,** holding scroll in l. hand, and with **r.** receiving ears **of corn** from Ceres r.; he is crowned by Victory, who stands behind him, wearing long doubled tunic and peplum, and holding with l. **hand palm** : border of dots.   Æ 2·65.   Pl. XII.

This medallion has a broad ornamented rim.

17. Obv. ANTONINVS AVG PIVS P P TR P XVIII Same type and border.

   Rev. COS IIII Hercules, facing, holding club and apple; on his l. arm hangs the lion's skin, and to his r. is the apple-tree of the Hesperides; Victory, advancing l., wearing doubled tunic, places wreath on his head with r. hand; she holds cornucopiæ with l.: border of dots.
   Æ 1·55. Pl. XIII. fig. 1.

18. Obv. ANTONINVS AVG PI VS P P TR P XVIII Head of Antoninus Pius r., laur.

   Rev. C O S I I I I Young Jupiter, seated sideways on the goat Amalthea walking r.
   Æ 1·1.

19. Obv. ANTONINVS AVG PIVS P P TR P XIX COS IIII Same type: border of dots.

   Rev. Silvanus, facing, mantle hanging on l. arm and falling over his knee; he rests l. arm on pillar, on the base of which he places his l. foot; with r. hand he holds falx, and with l. branch of oak, which he has just cut off a tree on his r.; at his feet, hound l. looking back, and on his l., garlanded altar, on which is a crater: border of dots.
   Æ 1·45. Pl. XIII. fig. 2.

20. Same, with broad ornamented rim.
   Æ 2·65.

21. Obv. ANTONINVS AVG PIVS P P IMP II Head of Antoninus Pius r., bare: border of dots.

   Rev. T R POT XXI C O S IIII Neptune, holding trident with l. hand, chlamys wrapped round his l. arm, advancing l., and conducting to a ship Ceres, whose veil floats over her head, and who carries ears of corn in the outer fold of her doubled tunic; behind them, a column surmounted by Priapic term: plain border.
   Æ 1·5. Pl. XIV. fig. 1.

22. Obv. ANTONINVS AVG PIVS P P TR P XXII Head of Antoninus Pius l., laur.: plain border.

   Rev. COS IIII (in exergue) The four Seasons represented by four children with attributes: they are all naked, with the exception of Winter; the first on the left, Spring r., bears on his head basket of flowers; the second, Summer r., holds falx and ears of corn; the third, Autumn l., holds fawn by the fore-legs and patera of fruit; the fourth, Winter l., hooded and wearing short tunic, carries hare, and over r. shoulder bent staff to the end of which is tied a bird: plain border.
   Æ 1·5. Pl. XIV. fig. 2.

ANTONINUS PIUS. 11

23. **Obv.** Same inscription. Head of Antoninus Pius r., bare : **border** of dots.

   Rev. [**VOT** SVSC]DEC II[I (In exergue ?) COS IIII] Emperor l., wearing **pontifical** robes, holding patera and scroll, and sacrificing at a lighted **tripod** ; before him, a camillus with patera in l. hand, a tibicen **r. playing** double flute, a victimarius, and a popa with axe raised felling an ox; the Emperor is accompanied by an attendant standing r. behind the tripod, **his r.** hand placed in the bosom of **his** toga.

   Æ 1·5.   Pl. XIV. fig. 3.

24. **Obv.** ANTONINVS AVG PI VS P P TR P XXIII   Bust of Antoninus **Pius** r., laur., wearing paludamentum and cuirass : border of dots.

   Rev. COS IIII (in exergue)   Jupiter, naked, in quadriga l., holding thunderbolt and sceptre ; horses walking : border of dots.

   Æ 1·55.   Pl. XV. fig. 1.

FAUSTINA THE ELDER.
Died a.d. 141.

1. Obv. **FAVSTINA AVG ANTONINI PII PP** Bust of Faustina r., draped; her hair is elaborately plaited, and arranged so as to terminate in a knot on the top of the head: border of dots.

    Rev. Cybele, turreted, wearing **tunic**, seated sideways on lion running r.; she holds tympanum with **r.** hand and sceptre with l.: border of dots.
    Æ 1·65. Pl. XVII. fig. 1.

2. Obv. **DIVA AVG FAVSTINA** Similar type, the head being veiled: border of dots.

    Rev. **AETER NITAS** Æternitas l., wearing stephane, tunic, and peplum; she holds on her r. hand a globe, surmounted by phœnix l., and rests her l. arm on a pillar, on the base of which she places her l. foot: border of dots.
    Æ 1·5. Pl. XV. fig. 2.

3. Obv. Same inscription and border. Similar type to no. 1.

    Rev. **SECV RITAS** Securitas, wearing stephane, and peplum over her knees, seated r. on a chair the arms of which are cornuacopiæ; on one of these she rests her r. elbow, supporting her head with r. hand; around her l. **arm** a serpent entwines itself: border of dots.
    Æ 1·5. Pl. XV. fig. 3.

4. Obv. **DIVA AVGVSTA FAVSTINA** Similar type: border of dots.

    Rev. Faustina? wearing tunic and peplum, stepping into biga l.; she holds the reins with both hands: plain border.
    Æ 2·6. Pl. XVI.

    This medallion has a **broad rim.**

5. Obv. Same inscription and border. Similar type to no. 2.

    Rev. Cybele, turreted, wearing tunic and peplum, seated sideways on lion walking l.; she holds with her r. hand reversed sceptre which passes over her shoulder, her l. hand rests on the back of the lion; behind her, a tree, from one of the branches of which hangs a pair of cymbals: border of dots.
    Æ 1·55. Pl. XVII. fig. 2.

6. Obv. **DIVA AVG FAVSTINA** Similar type: border of dots.

    Rev. Vulcan, wearing **short** tunic which **leaves his r.** shoulder bare, seated r., holding hammer with r. hand and with l. thunderbolt, which he has **forged on an anvil** placed upon **a stand**; against his seat rests a pair of tongs; **before** him, Minerva, helmeted, and wearing long doubled tunic, **standing** l. beneath **a tree,** her r. hand extended and her l. resting **on her** hip; behind **her,** shield ornamented with serpent: border **of dots.**
    Æ 1·6. Pl. XVII. fig. 3.

MARCUS AURELIUS.

(MARCVS AVRELIVS ANTONINVS, ARMENIACVS, PARTHICVS MAXIMVS, MEDICVS, GERMANICVS, SARMATICVS.)

CAES. A.D. 139 : AUG. A.D. 161 : DIED A.D. 180.

1. Obv. **AVRELIVS CAESAR AVG PII F COS** Bust of Marcus Aurelius r., bare-headed, wearing paludamentum : border of dots.

   Rev. Hercules r., seizing the centaur Nessus, whom he is striking with his club; behind him a tree, on which hangs the lion's skin: border of dots. Æ 1·5. Pl. XVIII. fig. 1.

2. Obv. **AVRELIVS CAESAR AVGVSTI PII F** Bust of Marcus Aurelius r., bare-headed, bearded, wearing paludamentum **and cuirass**: border of dots.

   Rev. Cæsar, wearing short tunic and mantle, on horse galloping r.; he hurls javelin at a wild boar running before him: border of dots. Æ 1·6. Pl. XVIII. fig. 3.

   The chronological place of this medallion is probably immediately after no. 5.

3. Obv. **AVRELIVS CAESAR AVG PII F TR P II COS II** Bust of Marcus Aurelius l., bare-headed, slightly **bearded, wearing** paludamentum : border of dots.

   Rev. **TEMPORVM FELI** (beneath) **CITAS** Hercules, the lion's skin on his l. shoulder, holding club and trophy, in chariot r., **drawn** by four centaurs, bearing the attributes of the four Seasons; **the** furthest **represents** Winter, hooded, bearing dried fruits and hare; **the** second, Spring, with basket **of** flowers on his shoulders ; **the** third, Summer, holding sickle and **ears of** corn ; and the fourth, Autumn, carrying pedum, on the end **of** which is the head of a **fawn**? border of dots. Æ 1·55. Pl. XVIII. fig. 2.

4. Obv. **AVRELIVS CAESAR AN TONINI AVG PII FIL** Bust of Marcus Aurelius l., bare-headed, slightly bearded, wearing cuirass : **border of dots.**

   Rev. **TR POT III COS II** Apollo towards r., hair long, wearing chlamys, holding strung **bow** with l., and quiver by the strap with r. ; before him, a tripod with three handles, on which hangs Python ; behind him, a table with two-handled **vase** upon it, and in the background a laurel, on which sits raven **r.** : border of dots. Æ 1·6. Pl. XIX. fig. 1.

5. Obv. AVRELIVSCAE SARAVGPIIFIL Bust of Marcus Aurelius r., bare-headed, slightly bearded, wearing paludamentum : border of dots.

Rev. [TRPOT]VIIII COSII Castor, a star above his head, wearing pileus and chlamys, walking l. by the side of his horse, on whose neck he places his r. hand, holding the bridle ; with his l. he carries spear : border of dots. Æ 1·6. Pl. XIX. fig. 2.

6. Obv. AVRELIVSCAES ANTONAVGPIIF Bust of Marcus Aurelius r., bare-headed, bearded, wearing paludamentum and cuirass : **border of** dots.

Rev. TRPOTXIII (In field) COSII Neptune l., resting r. foot on prow l., and leaning r. elbow on knee, over which hangs his chlamys ; he holds sceptre with l. hand, and extends r. towards Troy, of which the walls with a gateway are seen ; behind him, a dolphin l., in waves : border of dots. Æ 1·5. Pl. XIX. fig. 3.

7. Obv. MAVREL ANTONINVS AVG PM IMPII TRPXVIII COSIII Bust of Marcus Aurelius l., bare-headed, bearded, wearing paludamentum and cuirass : border of dots.

Rev. Female figure, wearing peplum which leaves r. side bare, standing r. beneath a laurel ; her l. leg is crossed in front of the r., and she rests her r. hand on a table, upon which are placed a vase, a laurel-garland, and a figure of Salus, around which a serpent entwines itself and feeds from the l. hand of the woman ; beneath, on the cross-bar of the table, a raven l. : border of dots. Æ 1·6. Pl. XX. fig. 1.

8. Obv. MAVREL ANTONINVS AVG ARME NIACVS PM IMPII TRP XIX COSIII Bust of Marcus Aurelius r., bearded and laur., wearing paludamentum and cuirass : border of dots.

Rev. Same. Æ 1·6.

9. Obv. MAVREL ANTONINVS AVG ARMENIACVS PM Bust of Marcus Aurelius l., bearded and laur., wearing cuirass : border of dots.

Rev. TRPXX IMPIII COSIII Minerva, helmeted, wearing sleeved tunic peplum and ægis, standing l. beneath an olivo ; she rests her l. hand on her hip, and with her r. feeds a serpent, which is coiled up on a garlanded altar ; behind her, a shield ; before her, on l. of altar, Victory r., wearing tunic, and holding vase and patera of fruit : border of dots. Æ 1·5. Pl. XX. fig. 2.

10. Obv. MANTONINVS AVG ARM PARTH MAX Bust of Marcus Aurelius r., bearded and laur., wearing paludamentum and cuirass : border of dots.

Rev. TRPXXII IMPIIII COSIII Colossal figure of Jupiter, towards l., holding thunderbolt and sceptre, and spreading out his pallium over Marcus Aurelius and Lucius Verus, who, each togato and holding scroll, stand on either side of him, and look towards him : border of dots. Æ 1·65. Pl. XXI. fig. 1.

11. Obv. Same.
   Rev. TR P XXIII IMP V COS III   Faustina? wearing stephane, tunic, and peplum, seated l. on throne, holding in l. hand sceptre, and extending r. to two genii advancing towards her and supporting between them a large cornucopiæ: border of dots.   Æ 1·5.   Pl. XXI. fig. 2.

12. Obv. M·ANTONINVS AVG TR P XXIIII-   Similar type l.: border of dots.
   Rev. PROFECTIO AVG (in exergue) COS III   Emperor, wearing paludamentum and cuirass, and holding spear couched, on horse cantering r.; he is accompanied by a horseman armed with spear, whose paludamentum floats behind him; they are preceded by a foot-soldier, looking back, who carries vexillum and shield, and are followed by another bearing signum: border of dots.   Æ 1·6.   Pl. XXII. fig. 1.

13. Obv. M ANTONINVS AVG TR P XXVII   Bust of Marcus Aurelius r., bearded and laur., wearing paludamentum and cuirass: border of dots.
   Rev. IMP VI COS III (In exergue) GERMANIA SVBACTA   Victory r., wearing doubled tunic; she holds palm with l. hand, and with r. inscribes shield attached to trophy, on r. of which stands the Emperor l., wearing paludamentum and cuirass, and holding spear in l.; at the base of the trophy are two captive Germans, seated back to back, of whom the one on l. is a woman, weeping, her hands clasped before her, the other, on r., a man, his hands bound behind him: border of dots.   Æ 1·5.   Pl. XXII. fig. 2.

14. Obv. M ANTONINVS AVG TR P XXVIII   Same type and border.
   Rev. IMP VI COS III (In exergue) VICT . GERM   Victory, wearing doubled tunic, in quadriga l.; she holds reins with r. hand, and looks back; horses walking: border of dots.   Æ 1·55.   Pl. XXII. fig. 3.

MARCUS AURELIUS AND COMMODUS.

Obv. M AVREL ANTONINVS AVG · L AVREL COMMODVS AVG   Busts, face to face, of Marcus Aurelius r. and Commodus l., each laur. and wearing paludamentum and cuirass; Marcus Aurelius is bearded: border of dots.

Rev. Mars, walking r., helmeted and wearing chlamys tied round the waist; he carries spear with r. hand, and trophy over l. shoulder: border of dots.   Æ 1·55.   Pl. XXIII. fig. 1.

FAUSTINA THE YOUNGER.

Mar. a.d. 145 ? Died a.d. 175.

1. Obv. **FAVSTINA AVG PII AVG FIL** Bust of Faustina r., draped, her hair wavy and plaited in a knot at the back of the head: border of dots.

    Rev. Diana, wearing short tunic, standing r. before a fountain flowing down a rock, throwing off her peplum; at her feet, a hound r. drinking at the fountain; upon the rock, a tree; behind the goddess, another rock on which hangs the hide of a deer, and beneath which, on the ground, are her unstrung bow and quiver: border of dots.
    Æ 1·6. Pl. XXIII. fig. 3.

    This medallion is much tooled, and the lower part of the tree has been altered to a Priapic term: this is evident from comparison with a medallion of Antoninus Pius, having the same reverse, in the Imperial Museum at Vienna. (Num. Cim. Austr. Vind. i. (pl.) p. 35. no. II.)

2. Obv. Similar.

    Rev. Venus Genetrix? standing, facing, in a garden; she wears peplum; with r. hand she plucks a branch from a tree; a naked child runs to her l. side; around her are five Cupids, two of whom are playing on a suggestum beneath the tree; two others are flying down from a battlemented wall, on the r., and the fifth runs r.; above the wall are seen the tops of trees: border of dots.
    Æ 1·65. Pl. XXIV. fig. 1.

3. Obv. Similar.

    Rev. Isis Sothis, with usual headdress, wearing tunic and peplum, seated sideways on the Dog running r. and looking back; she holds sistrum with r. hand and sceptre with l.: border of dots.
    Æ 1·2. Pl. XXIV. fig. 2.

4. Obv. **FAVSTINA AVGVSTA** Similar type l.: border of dots.

    Rev. Isis l., with usual headdress, wearing tunic and peplum; she holds sistrum with r. hand and ears of corn? with l.; at her feet in front, peacock displayed, and behind, lion advancing r. looking back: border of dots.
    Æ 1·3. Pl. XXIV. fig. 3.

5. Obv. Same as no. 1.

    Rev. Peacock displayed: border of dots.
    Æ 1·6.

FAUSTINA THE YOUNGER.

6. Obv. **FAVSTINA AVGVSTA** Similar type: same border.
   Rev. **Venus** r., wearing tunic and peplum, holding **sceptre with r. hand and dove on l.**: border of dots. Æ 1·25. Pl. XXIV. fig. 4.

7. Obv. Same inscription and border, and similar type l.
   Rev. **Vesta, veiled,** wearing stephane, tunic, and peplum, **seated l. on throne, her feet** on footstool; **she** holds sceptre **with l. hand, and with r. receives a** small group, **representing** the three **Graces, from Faustina, standing before her, wearing tunic and peplum**: border of dots.
   Æ 1·55. Pl. XXIV. fig. 5.

8. Obv. **DIVA FAV STINA PIA** Similar type: **border of** dots.
   Rev. **SIDERIBVS REC EPTA** Faustina in **the** character of Diana, as Hecate, r., wearing doubled tunic and drapery floating behind from her waist; she holds **with** both hands a long flaming torch; behind her neck is **a crescent, and slung to her** shoulders, her quiver; before her, **a garlanded lighted altar: border of dots.**
   Æ 1·6. Pl. XXIII. fig. 2.

LUCIUS VERUS.

(LVCIVS AVRELIVS VERVS, ARMENIACVS, **PARTHICVS** MAXIMVS, MEDICVS.)

Aug. A.D. 161 : Died A.D. 169.

1. Obv. L VERVS AVG ARM PARTH MAX   Bust of Lucius Verus l., laur., wearing cuirass: border of dots.

    Rev. TR P VI IMP III COS II   Emperor l., wearing paludamentum and cuirass, and armed with parazonium, leaning with l. hand on spear, and receiving with r. wreath, which Victory r., wearing doubled tunic, presents to him with both hands : border of dots.

    Æ 1·55.   Pl. XXV. fig. 1.

2. Obv. Same inscription.   Bust of Lucius Verus l., laur., wearing paludamentum and cuirass: border of dots.

    Rev. TR P VII IMP IIII (in exergue) COS III   Marcus Aurelius and Lucius Verus, each holding laurel-branch and sceptre, in triumphal quadriga l., conducted by Roma, carrying shield and vexillum, and preceded by a captive king, wearing tiara ; the horses are walking ; the chariot is ornamented with reliefs ; in the background, a trophy, supported by four soldiers ; at the base of the trophy, two captives seated back to back, their hands tied behind them : border of dots.

    Æ 1·5.   Pl. XXV. fig. 2.

3. Obv. Same.

    Rev. TR P VIII IMP IIII COS III   Colossal figure of Jupiter towards l., holding thunderbolt and sceptre, and spreading out his pallium over Marcus Aurelius and Lucius Verus, who, togate, are standing one on either side of him, and are looking towards him ; each holds sceptre and scroll : border of dots.   Æ 1·6.

4. Obv. L VERVS AVG ARM   PARTH MAX   Bust of Lucius Verus r., laur., wearing paludamentum and cuirass: border of dots.

    Rev. Similar.   Æ 1·7.   Pl. XXV. fig. 3.

5. Obv. L VERVS AVG ARM   PARTH MAX TR P VIIII   Similar type: border of dots.

    Rev. COS III (in exergue)   Roma, helmeted and wearing short doubled tunic which leaves r. breast bare, seated l. on cuirass, and presenting olive-branch ? to the Emperor, standing r. before her, helmeted, clad in paludamentum and cuirass, and holding with l. hand spear ; Roma is crowned by Victory, who, wearing doubled tunic, stands behind her, and holds with l. hand palm : border of dots.   Æ 1·55.

LUCILLA.

Mar. a.d. 164 : Died a.d. 183 ?

1. Obv. LVCILLAE AVG ANTONINI AVG F Bust of Lucilla r., draped; her hair wavy and plaited in a knot at the back of the head: border of dots.

   Rev. Ceres, veiled and wearing tunic, seated r. on cista around which serpent entwines itself; she holds long torch with l. hand, and with r. presents ears of corn to Lucilla l., wearing tunic and peplum, her l. arm resting on column: border of dots. Æ 1·6.   Pl. XXVI. fig. 1.

2. Obv. LVCILLA AVGVSTA Similar type l., with roll of hair worn as a diadem: border of dots.

   Rev. Cybele, turreted, wearing tunic and peplum, seated sideways on lion running r.; with r. hand she holds tympanum ornamented with star, and in l. sceptre: border of dots.   Æ 1·55.   Pl. XXVI. fig. 2.

3. Obv. Same inscription and border as no. 1, and similar type.

   Rev. Six veiled women, standing on r. and l. of a garlanded and lighted altar, which is in front of the Temple of Vesta; one of them, on r. of altar, is sacrificing, and holds in r. hand patera, and in l. acerra; the temple is of the circular peripteral form, four columns of the peristyle being shown; the statue of Vesta is seen in the cella: border of dots.   Æ 1·7.   Pl. XXVI. fig. 3.

COMMODUS AND ANNIUS VERUS.

1. Obv. **COMMODVS** CAES · **VERVS** CAES. Youthful busts, face to face, of Commodus and Annius **Verus**; each is bareheaded, and wears paludamentum: border of dots.

   Rev. TEMPORVM (in exergue) The four Seasons, represented **by four FELICITAS**
   children **with attributes**; they are all naked, with the exception of Winter; the first on the left, Spring r., bears on his shoulders basket of flowers; the second, Summer r., holds falx and ears of corn; the third, Autumn l., holds by the fore-legs fawn, and patera of fruit; the fourth, Winter l., hooded and wearing short tunic, carries hare, and over r. shoulder bent staff, to the end of which is tied a brace of birds: border of dots.   Æ 1·7.   Pl. XXVII. fig. 1.

2.   Same.   Æ 1·5.

COMMODUS.

(MARCVS LVCIVS AELIVS AVRELIVS COMMODVS ANTONINVS, GERMANICVS, SARMATICVS, BRITANNICVS, HERCVLEVS.)

CAES. A.D. 166: AUG. A.D. 177: DIED A.D. 192.

1. Obv. IMP CAES L AVREL COM MODVS GERM SARM   Youthful bust of Commodus r., laur., wearing ægis: border of dots.

    Rev. TR POT COS (in exergue)   Marcus Aurelius and Commodus, each holding laurel-branch, in triumphal quadriga l., conducted by Roma, looking back, helmeted and carrying spear; the horses are walking; the chariot is ornamented with reliefs; above quadriga, Victory flying l. with trophy and palm: border of dots.

    Æ 1·55. Pl. XXVII. fig. 2.

2. Obv. Same.

    Rev. TR POT COS   Hercules, standing towards l., holding club and apple; on his l. arm hangs the lion's skin; Victory, advancing l., wearing doubled tunic, places wreath on his head with r. hand, and holds cornucopiæ with l.: border of dots.

    Æ 1·6.

3. Obv. L AVREL COMMODVS AVG GERM SARM TR P III   Bust of Commodus r., laur., wearing paludamentum and cuirass: border of dots.

    Rev. IMP II COS PP (In exergue) VOTA PVBLICA   Emperor l., wearing pontifical robes, holding patera and scroll, and sacrificing at a lighted tripod, placed in front of a hexastyle temple of the Corinthian order; he is accompanied by four priests, behind whom are two standards; before him, on l. of tripod, a camillus, a tibicen playing double flute, a soldier with spear, and a popa with uplifted axe felling an ox; the tympanum of the pediment of the temple is ornamented with a standing figure of Jupiter holding sceptro, on his r. an eagle, and on his l. a kneeling figure; on each of the angles of the pediment is a Victory, and on the apex, a group of figures.

    Æ 1·5. Pl. XXVII. fig. 3.

4. Obv. LAVREL COMMODVS AVG GERM SARM TR P IIII Same type and border.

Rev. IMP IIII COS II P P Female figure, wearing peplum which leaves r. side bare, standing r. beneath a laurel, her l. leg crossed in front of the r., and leaning with r. hand on a table, upon which are placed a vase, a laurel-garland, and a figure of Salus, around which a serpent entwines itself and feeds from the l. hand of the woman; beneath, on the cross-bar of the table, a raven l.: border of dots. Æ 1·6.

This medallion is much tooled, and the inscription IMP IIII, on the rev., appears to have been altered from IMP II, which is found in the specimen published by Cohen. (Monnaies Impériales, vol. iii., p. 107, no. 367.) Commodus did not receive the title IMP IIII till he had reached his fifth tribunitian year.

5. Obv. LAVREL COMMODVS AVG GERM SARM TR P V⁻ Same type and border.

Rev. IMP III COS II P P Victory, wearing doubled tunic and peplum, towards l., looking back; she leans with l. arm on pillar, and rests her l. foot on its base, holding wreath and palm: border of dots.
Æ 1·6.

6. Obv. M·AVREL·COMMODVS ANTONINVS·AVG Bust of Commodus r., bearded and laur., wearing paludamentum and cuirass: border of dots.

Rev. TR P VIII IMP V COS IIII P P Emperor l., wearing paludamentum and cuirass, and armed with parazonium, leaning with l. hand on spear, and receiving with r. wreath, which Victory r., clad in doubled tunic, presents to him with both hands. Æ 1·5. Pl. XXVIII. fig. 1.

7. Obv. M·AVREL COMMODVS ANTONINVS AVG Bust of Commodus r., bearded and laur., wearing paludamentum and cuirass: border of dots.

Rev. TR P VIII·IMP V (in exergue) Roma, helmeted, and wearing tunic
COS IIII P P
and peplum, seated r., holding Victory and sceptre; before her, Fortuna, seated l., in the same dress, holding rudder and cornucopiæ; between them, a lighted tripod at which the Emperor l., in pontifical robes and holding patera, is sacrificing; before him, on l. of tripod, a camillus r. with acerra, and a tibicen r. playing double flute: border of dots. Æ 1·65. Pl. XXVIII. fig. 2.

8. Obv. Similar inscription and type, and same border.

Rev. TR P VIII IM P V COS IIII P P (In exergue) VIRTVTI AVG Virtus, helmeted, and wearing tunic which leaves r. breast bare and peplum, seated l. on cuirass, looking back; she holds spear with raised r. hand and parazonium with l., and rests l. arm on shield ornamented with Wolf and Twins; before her, trophy: border of dots. Æ 1·5.

COMMODUS.

9. Obv. **M·AVREL·COMMODVS ANTONINVS AVG PIVS** Similar type: same border.

    Rev. **PM TR P VIIII·IMP VI** (in exergue) **COS IIII P P** Jupiter, wearing pallium, seated r. on throne, his feet on footstool; he holds sceptro with raised l. hand, and with r. presents globe to the Emperor, standing before him, togate: border of dots. Æ 1·5. Pl. XXVIII. fig. 3.

10. Obv. **M-AVREL COMMODVS ANTONINVS AVG** Similar type.

    Rev. [**TR P**] **VIIII** [**IMP VI**] (In exergue) [**COS IIII P P**] Jupiter, holding sceptre with r. hand, standing, facing, head r., between Juno and Minerva; with l. hand he holds r. of Juno, who stands l., veiled, wearing doubled tunic and **peplum, and** holding sceptre; Minerva, helmeted, and wearing **tunic and peplum**, stands r., with spear in r. hand, her l. **resting on shield.** Æ 1·5.

11. Obv. **M-AVREL-COMMODVS ANTONINVS AVG PIVS** Same type.

    Rev. **PM-TR P VIIII-IMP VI-COS IIII P-P** Minerva, helmeted, and clad in tunic ægis and peplum, seated l. on throne, her feet on footstool; on r. hand she holds Victory l., and with raised l. spear; at her side, resting against the throne, is her shield, ornamented with head of Medusa: border of dots. Æ 1·55. Pl. XXIX. fig. 1.

12. Obv. **M·COMMODVS·ANTONI NVS AVG PIVS BRIT** Bust of Commodus r., bearded and laur., wearing paludamentum and cuirass: border of dots.

    Rev. **BRITTANIA PM TR P X IMP VII COS IIII P P** Britannia Romana, wearing short tunic mantle and braceæ, seated l. on rock; she holds standard with r. hand and spear with l., **and her l.** arm rests upon an oval shield, having spike in centre and beaded border, which is placed on helmet r.: border of dots. Æ 1·65. Pl. XXIX. fig. 2.

13. Obv. **M·COMMODVS·ANTONI NVS·AVG·PIVS·BRIT** Same type as no. 11: border of dots.

    Rev. **PM TR P X IMP VII COS IIII P P** Emperor l., wearing paludamentum and cuirass, his r. foot resting on helmet; he holds on r. hand globe surmounted by Victory r., and with l. spear, reversed: border of dots. Æ 1·5.

    This medallion is struck in two metals.

14. Obv. M‑COMMODVS‑ANTO NINVS‑AVG‑PIVS‑BRIT Bust of Commodus r., bearded and laur., wearing paludamentum and cuirass: border of dots.

   Rev. ‑P‑M‑TR P X IMP VII COS IIII‑P‑P Hercules, facing; with his r. hand he crowns himself, and with his l. holds club; on l. arm hangs the lion's skin; to l. is a tree, on one of the boughs of which hang bow-case and quiver; to r., a garlanded lighted altar: border of dots. Æ 1·5. Pl. XXX. fig. 1.

   This medallion is struck in two metals.

15. Obv. M COMMODVS ANTO NINVS AVG PIVS BRIT Bust of Commodus r., bearded and laur., wearing paludamentum: border of dots.

   Rev. P M TR P X IMP VII COS IIII P·P Jupiter r., wearing pallium, holding globe and sceptre with l. hand, and resting r. on a circle, within which are four female figures, representing the Seasons; each one wears doubled tunic and bears the attribute of the season she personifies; the foremost, Spring, holds the end of her veil with r. hand and basket with l.; the second, Summer, falx; the third, Autumn, bunch of grapes; and the fourth, Winter, who is hooded, staff over r. shoulder; before Jupiter, a genius l. bearing with both hands cornucopiæ on r. shoulder border of dots.
   Æ 1·6. Pl. XXX. fig. 2.

16. Obv. M COMMODVS ANTONI NVS AVG PIVS BRIT Bust of Commodus r., bearded and laur., wearing paludamentum and cuirass.

   Rev. P M TR P X IMP [VII COS IIII] Victory, wearing peplum, seated r. on cuirass; she holds with r. hand palm, and with l. shield, which rests upon her l. knee, and bears the inscription $\frac{VICT}{BRIT}$; before her, trophy; behind her, shield. Æ 1·5. Pl. XXXI. fig. 1.

17. Obv. M COMMODVS ANTO NINVS AVG PIVS BRIT Similar type.

   Rev. P M T R P X IMP VII COS IIII Similar type. Æ 1·55.

18. Obv. M COMMODVS ANTONINVS PIVS FELIX AVG BRIT Similar type: border of dots.

   Rev. FORTV NAE REDVCI (In exergue) C·V·P·P Emperor r., wearing pontifical robes, and holding patera and scroll, sacrificing at a lighted tripod, placed before Fortuna, who is seated l. on throne, wearing stephane tunic and peplum, and holding rudder and cornucopiæ: border of dots. Æ 1·55. Pl. XXXI. fig. 2.

19. Obv. M COMMODVS ANTONINV S PIVS FELIX AVG BRIT   Bust of Commodus l., bearded and laur., holding spear with r. hand, and wearing ægis : border of dots.

Rev. P M T R P XI (In exergue) COS V P P   Emperor, in triumphal quadriga r., extending r. hand and holding sceptre surmounted by eagle with l. ; horses walking ; the chariot is ornamented with reliefs representing the Emperor crowned by Victory and a figure reclining l. border of dots.   Æ 1·55.   Pl. XXXI. fig. 3.

20. Obv. M COMMODVS · ANTONINVS · PIVS · FELIX · AVG BRIT   Januiform bust, clad in paludamentum and cuirass, of Commodus r. and Janus l., both bearded and laur. : border of dots.

Rev. P M · T R P · XII · IMP VIII CO S V P P (In exergue) TELLVS STABIL   Tellus, wearing peplum, reclining l. ; she rests her l. arm on basket filled with fruit, and holds with her l. hand long vine-branch from which hangs bunch of grapes ; her r. hand is placed on globo, studded with stars, around which pass four female figures, each clad in doubled tunic, representing the seasons with their attributes : border of dots.   Æ 1·55.   Pl. XXXII. fig. 1.

21. Obv. M COMMODVS ANTONINVS PIVS FELIX AVG BRIT   Bust of Commodus r., bearded and laur., wearing paludamentum and cuirass.

Rev. P M T R P XII IMP VIII (In exergue) TELLVS STABIL   Similar type.
C O S V P P   Æ 1·5.

22. Obv. M COMMODVS ANTONI NVS PIVS FELIX AVG BRIT   Bust of Commodus r., bearded and laur., wearing paludamentum and cuirass : border of dots.

Rev. P M T R P XII IMP VIII COS V (In exergue) PROVID AVG   Ship in full sail l. ; beneath, waves : border of dots.
Æ 1·6.   Pl. XXXII. fig. 2.

23. Obv. M COMMODVS ANTONINVS PIVS FELIX · AVG BRIT ·   Bust of Commodus l., bearded and laur., wearing paludamentum and cuirass ; over r. shoulder, the parazonium-strap : border of dots.

Rev. P M · T R P XIII · IMP VIII (In exergue) COS V P P   Salus, wearing tunic and peplum, seated l. on throne ; she holds patera with r. hand, feeding a serpent which rises from an altar before her ; on l. of altar, Hilaritas r., who wears stephane tunic and peplum, and holds long palm and cornucopiæ : border of dots.
Æ 1·6.   Pl. XXXIII. fig. 1.

This medallion is struck in two metals, the rim being of a lighter colour.

24. Obv. M COMMODVS [ANTONINVS] PIVS FELIX AVG BRIT Bust of Commodus r., bearded and laur., wearing paludamentum and cuirass: border of dots.

Rev. IOV IVVENI PM T R P XIIII IMP VIII (In exergue) COS V PP Jupiter l., his chlamys hanging on l. arm, holding thunderbolt with r. hand, and sceptre with l.; behind him, eagle r. looking back; before him, altar ornamented with relief apparently representing the god slaying a giant: border of dots. Æ 1·6.

This medallion is struck in two metals.

25. Obv. M COMMODVS ANTONINVS PIVS FELIX AVG BRIT Same type and border.

Rev. MA RT PACAT PM T RP XIIII IMP VIII COS V PP Mars l., helmeted, his chlamys hanging on l. arm, holding olive-branch with r. hand, and reversed spear with l.; before him, shield and greaves; behind him, cuirass: border of dots. Æ 1·5.

This medallion has been gilt.

26. Obv. M COMMODVS ANTONINVS PIVS FELIX · AVG BRIT · Bust of Commodus l., bearded and laur., wearing paludamentum and cuirass; over r. shoulder is the parazonium-strap: border of dots.

Rev. MINER VICT PM TR P XIIII IMP VIII (In exergue) COS V PP Minerva l., helmeted, wearing tunic regis and peplum; she leans with l. hand on reversed spear, and holds on r. Victory bearing wreath and palm; at her feet, a shield ornamented with armed figures; behind her, a trophy at the base of which are two shields: border of dots. Æ 1·6. Pl. XXXIII. fig. 2.

This medallion is struck in two metals, the rim being of a lighter colour.

27. Obv. M - COMMODVS ANTONINVS PIVS - FELIX - AVG - BRIT Bust of Commodus r., bearded and laur., wearing paludamentum and cuirass: border of dots.

Rev. MINER - VICT - P M - TR P XIIII IMP VIII (In exergue) COS V PP Similar type; the shield at the feet of Minerva being ornamented with rays: border of dots. Æ 1·5.

28. Obv. M COMMODVS ANTONINVS PIVS FELIX AVG BRIT Bust of Commodus l., bearded and laur., wearing cuirass.

Rev. SECVRIT PVB P M TR P XIIII IMP VIII (In exergue) COS V P P Securitas, wearing peplum, seated l. on throne, her feet resting on footstool; she holds globe on her r. hand. Æ 1·55.

COMMODUS.

29. Obv. M COMMODVS ANTONINVS PIVS FELIX AVG BRIT   Bust of Commodus r., bearded and laur., wearing paludamentum and cuirass: border of dots.

   Rev. **COS VI** (in exergue)   Emperor r., wearing paludamentum and cuirass, holding parazonium with r. hand, and leaning with l. on reversed spear; before him, Africa, reclining l., her r. leg crossed over the l., wearing peplum and head-dress of elephant's skin; she places her r. hand on the back of a lion l., and holds with her l. ears of corn; in the background, Victory r. erecting a trophy: border of dots.
   Æ 1·55.   Pl. XXXIII. fig. 3.

   This medallion is struck in two metals, the rim being of a lighter colour.

30. Obv. [Same inscription.]   Bust of Commodus l., bearded and laur., wearing paludamentum and cuirass; over r. shoulder, the parazonium-strap.

   Rev. [PIO IMP OMNIA FELICIA PM TRP XV IMP VIII]   (In exergue) **COS VI PP**   Neptune r., his l. foot on prow r.; he holds trident with r. hand and dolphin on l., and rests l. elbow on knee over which hangs his chlamys; before him, lighted altar at which the Emperor l., wearing pontifical robes and holding patera and scroll, is sacrificing.   Æ 1·5.

   The edge of this medallion has been hammered, and the inscriptions around thus rendered illegible.

31. Obv. IMP COMMODVS AVG·PIVS·FELIX   Bust of Commodus r., bearded and laur., wearing paludamentum and cuirass: border of dots.

   Rev. **PM TR P XV·IMP VIII** (In exergue) **COS VI P·P·**   Emperor in triumphal quadriga l., horses walking; he extends his r. hand, and holds sceptre surmounted by eagle with l.; behind him, Victory crowning him with wreath; the chariot is ornamented with relief representing Victory bearing palm: border of dots.
   Æ 1·6.   Pl. XXXIV. fig. 1.

32. Obv. M COMMODVS ANTONI NVS PIVS FELIX AVG BRIT   Bust of Commodus r., bearded and laur., wearing paludamentum and cuirass: border of dots.

   Rev. **PM TR P[XVI IMP] VIII** (In exergue) **COS VI PP**   Roma, helmeted and wearing peplum, seated l. on cuirass against which rests shield; she holds cornucopiæ with l. hand, and with r. presents globe surmounted by Palladium to the Emperor standing before her, togate; between them, in the background, Felicitas l., veiled, and holding winged caduceus; behind the Emperor, Victory r., wearing doubled tunic, holding palm, and crowning him with wreath: border of dots.
   Æ 1·65.

   This medallion is struck in two metals.

33. Obv. L·AELIVS·AVRELIVS·COMMO DVS AVG PIVS FELIX Heads, jugate, r., of Commodus, bearded laur. and radiate, and Amazon, (Marcia?) wearing crested helmet and necklace below which, pelta: border of dots.

Rev. PM TR P XVII · IMP VIII COS VII P P Emperor l., wearing pontifical robes; he holds patera and scroll, and sacrifices at a garlanded and lighted altar; on the other side of the altar, Hercules r., in an attitude of repose, the r. hand on the hip, the l. holding club which rests upon a rock; over the l. arm hangs the lion's skin: border of dots. Æ 1·7. Pl. XXXIV. fig. 2.

This medallion is struck in two metals, the rim being of a darker colour.

34. Obv. L AELIVS AVRELIVS COM MODVS AVG PIVS FELIX Bust of Commodus, as Hercules, r., bearded and laur., wearing lion's skin tied in a knot in front: border of dots.

Rev. PM TR P XVII IMP V III COS VII P P Similar type: border of dots. Æ 1·6.

This medallion is struck in two metals, the rim being of a lighter colour.

35. Obv. L AELIVS AVRELIVS CO MMODVS AVG PIVS FEL Bust of Commodus r., bearded and laur., wearing paludamentum and cuirass: border of dots.

Rev. [PM TR P X VII IMP VIII] (In exergue) COS VII P P Felicitas, facing, head r., wearing tunic and peplum; she holds long caduceus and cornucopiæ, and stands between the Emperor l., wearing pontifical robes, holding patera and scroll, and sacrificing at a lighted tripod, and a popa r., leading bull with l. hand, and carrying axe in r. Æ 1·6.

36. Obv. L AEL·AVREL·CO MM·AVG·P FEL Bust of Commodus r., bearded and laur., wearing paludamentum: border of dots.

Rev. P M TR P XVII IMP VIII (In exergue) COS VII P P Similar type: border of dots. Æ 1·1. Pl. XXXIV. fig. 3.

37. Obv. L AELIVS AVRELIVS COMMODVS AVG PIVS FELIX Head of Commodus, as Hercules, r., bearded, and wearing lion's skin: border of dots.

Rev. HERCVLI ROMANO AVG PM TR P XVIII COS VII P P Emperor, as Hercules, l., bearded and laur., holding with l. hand by the strap case containing bow and arrows, and resting r. on his club; before him, on a rock, the boar's skin; and behind him, on another rock, that of the lion. Æ 1·65. Pl. XXXIV. fig. 4.

This medallion is struck in two metals.

COMMODUS.

38. Obv. L AELIVS·AVRELIVS·C OMMODVS·AVG PIVS·FELIX Similar type l.

    Rev. **Same.** Æ 1·6.

39. Obv. **L AELIVS** AVRELIVS COMMODVS AVG PIVS FELIX Similar type r. : border of dots.

    Rev. [**HERCVLI**] ROMANO AVG P M TR P XVIII COS VII P P Emperor, as Hercules, bearded and laur., standing r., in an attitude of repose, **resting** his r. hand on his hip, and leaning with l. arm on his club, which is placed on a rock, and is partly covered by the lion's skin ; with the l. hand he holds strung bow : border of dots.

    Æ 1·65. Pl. XXXV. fig. 1.

    This medallion is struck in two metals, the rim being **of a** lighter **colour.**

40. Obv. L **AELIVS AVRELIVS COMMODVS AVG PIVS FELIX** Similar type l. : **border of dots.**

    Rev. Same. Æ 1·6.

41. Obv. L·AELIVS·AVRELIVS·COMMODVS AVG PIVS FELIX Same type and border.

    Rev. **HERC·ROM·CONDITORI·P M TR P** [XVIII] (In exergue) **COS VII·P·P** Emperor, as Hercules, bearded, and wearing **on** the head lion's skin which passes round l. arm ; he guides with **r.** hand and foot plough l., drawn by yoke of oxen ; with l. hand he holds club border of dots. Æ 1·55. Pl. XXXV. fig. 2.

42. Obv. L·AELIVS·AVRELIVS·COMMODVS·AVG PIVS·FELIX Same type r. : border of dots.

    Rev. **HERC ROM CONDITORI P M T R P XVIII** (In exergue) **COS VII P·P·** Same type. Æ 1·6.

    This medallion is struck in two metals.

43. Obv. Same type.

    Rev. **HERCVLI ROMANO AVGV** Bow strung, club, and quiver full of arrows. Æ 2·55. Pl. XXXVI.

    This medallion has a thick ornamented rim.

44. Obv. IMP·COMMODVS·AVG·PIVS·FELIX   Bust of Commodus r., bearded and laur., wearing paludamentum : border of dots.

Rev. VOTIS FELICIBVS   Emperor l., wearing pontifical robes, and holding patera and scroll, sacrificing at a tripod placed at the entrance of a harbour, towards which three galleys and two small boats are seen approaching in the following order; first, a galley containing four soldiers, and having at the prow two military standards ; behind it, a vessel in full sail, having vexillum at the prow, piloted by Jupiter Serapis who is seated at the stern ; above, a similar vessel in full sail, preceded by small boat with single oarsman ; below, another small boat with single oarsman, and near it, buoy ? The Emperor is accompanied by a priest who stands behind the tripod ; behind the Emperor, a pharos, and beneath, on the sea-shore, a slain bull : border of dots.   Æ 1·6. Pl. XXXV. fig. 3.

This medallion is struck in two metals, the rim being of a lighter colour.

45. Obv. IMP COMMODVS AVG PIVS FELIX   Bust of Commodus, full face, bearded and laur., wearing paludamentum and cuirass.

Rev. Same inscription and similar type.   Æ 2·2.

This medallion is struck in two metals : the rim is loose.

46. Obv. COMMODVS ANTONINVS PIVS [FELIX AVG BRIT]   Bust of Commodus l., bearded and laur., wearing paludamentum and cuirass ; over r. shoulder, the parazonium-strap.

Rev. Same inscription and similar type.   Æ 1·65.

This medallion is struck in two metals, the rim being of a lighter colour.

COMMODUS AND CRISPINA.

Mar. a.d. 177.

Obv. IMP COMMODVS AVG GERM SARM CRISPINA AVG Busts, face to face, of Commodus l., laur., wearing paludamentum and cuirass, and Crispina r., draped, her hair wavy and plaited in a knot at the back of the head : border of dots.

Rev. VOTA PVBLICA Commodus r., togate, clasping with his r. hand the r. hand of Crispina l., veiled and wearing tunic ; between them, Concordia, facing, veiled and wearing tunic and peplum, and resting a hand on the shoulder of each : border of dots.

Æ 1·6.   Pl. XXXVII. fig. 1.

SEPTIMIUS SEVERUS.

(LVCIVS SEPTIMIVS SEVERVS PERTINAX, ARABICVS, ADIABENICVS, PARTHICVS MAXIMVS, BRITANNICVS.)

Aug. A.D. 193: Died A.D. 211.

1. Obv. L SEPTIMIVS SEVERVS PERTINAX AVG PIVS Bust of Septimius Severus l., laur., carrying spear and shield with boss: border of dots.

   Rev. P M TR P III COS II P P (In exergue) FIDEI MILIT Emperor, wearing paludamentum and cuirass, and holding sceptre with l. hand, standing l. on a suggestum, and addressing six soldiers who are drawn up in two ranks before him; the three soldiers of the front rank hold shields, and those of the rear rank, three standards, a vexillum, aquila, and signum; the Emperor is accompanied by Caracalla and Geta, wearing tunics and paludamenta, standing behind him on the suggestum: border of dots. Æ 1·65. Pl. XXXVII. fig. 2.

2. Obv. L SEPTIMIVS SEVERVS PERTINAX AVG IMP III Bust of Septimius Severus r., laur., wearing paludamentum and cuirass.

   Rev. DIS AVSPICIBVS P M TR P [III] COS II P P Hercules and Bacchus l.: the former rests r. hand on his club, and carries lion's skin on l. arm: the latter holds cantharus with r. hand and thyrsus bound with fillet in l.; before him, panther l. looking back. Æ 1·65.

3. Obv. L SEPTIMIVS SEVERVS PERTINAX AVG IMP IIII Similar type.

   Rev. P·M·TR P·III COS·II·P·P· (In exergue) FIDEI MILIT Similar type to no. 1. Æ 1·6. Pl. XXXVII. fig. 3.

4. Obv. [L SEPTIMIVS SEVERVS PERTINAX AVG IMP IIII] Bust of Septimius Severus r., laur., wearing paludamentum and cuirass ornamented with head of Medusa: border of dots.

   Rev. V[ICT] AVG TR P [III COS II PP] Victory, wearing doubled tunic, running r., holding wreath with outstretched r. hand, and palm with l.: border of dots. Æ 1·7.

SEPTIMIUS SEVERUS. 33

5. Obv. L SEPTIMIVS SEVERVS PERTINAX AVG IMP VIII Bust of Septimius Severus r., laur., wearing paludamentum and cuirass: border of dots.

   Rev. [DIVI M PII F] P M TR P IIII COS II P P Roma l., helmeted and wearing short doubled tunic and chlamys over l. arm; she holds parazonium with r. hand, and leans with l. on spear; behind her, at her feet, shield: border of dots.   Æ 1·65.

JULIA DOMNA.

Mar. a.d. 173: Died a.d. 217.

1. Obv. IVLIA AVGVSTA   Bust of Julia Domna r., draped, her hair wavy, covering the ears, and plaited in a large flat knot behind the head.

    Rev. C E [R E] S   Ceres l., wearing stephane veil and doubled tunic; she holds ears of corn and long torch; before her, a garlanded altar.
    Æ 1·5.

2. Obv. Same inscription and similar type: border of dots.

    Rev. FECVN DITATI AVG   Julia Domna, as Fecunditas, wearing stephane tunic and peplum, seated r. on throne; she is suckling a babe; (Geta;) at her feet, a child (Caracalla) l., wearing toga pretexta: border of dots.   Æ 1·6.   Pl. XXXVII. fig. 4.

CARACALLA.

(MARCVS AVRELIVS ANTONINVS, PARTHICVS MAXIMVS, BRITANNICVS, GERMANICVS.)

CAES. A.D. 196: AVG. A.D. 198: DIED A.D. 217.

Obv. M AVRELIVS AN TONINVS CAES Youthful bust of Caracalla r., bare-headed, wearing paludamentum: **border** of dots.

Rev. SEVERI AVG PII FIL Instruments of sacrifice; lituus, secespita, patera, præfericulum, simpulum, and "aspergillum": border of dots. Æ 1·55.

GETA.

(LVCIVS PVBLIVS SEPTIMIVS GETA, BRITANNICVS.)

CAES. A.D. 198 ; AUG. A.D. 209 ; DIED A.D. 212.

Obv. P SEPTIMIVS GETA CAESAR Bust of Geta l., bare-headed and slightly bearded, wearing paludamentum and cuirass, and holding with r. hand spear ? over shoulder : border of dots.

Rev. CON COR DIA (In exergue) MILITVM Geta l., wearing paludamentum and cuirass, and holding spear ? with l. hand ; before him, three signa, the nearest of which, surmounted by Victory, he grasps with r. hand ; behind him, aquila and signum : border of dots.

Æ 1·65.   Pl. XXXVIII. fig. 1.

ELAGABALUS.

(MARCVS AVRELIVS ANTONINVS.)

Aug. a.d. 218 : Died a.d. 222.

Obv. **IMP CAES M** AVR ANTONINVS PIVS AVG   Bust of Elagabalus r., **laur.**, wearing paludamentum and cuirass : border of dots.

Rev. [AE]QVITAS AVGVSTI   The three Monetæ l., each holding scales and cornucopiæ, and having at her feet a conical heap of metal : **border of dots.**   Æ 1·25.   Wt. 308·5 grs.   Pl. XXXVIII. fig. 2.

SEVERUS ALEXANDER.

(MARCVS AVRELIVS SEVERVS ALEXANDER.)

CAES. A.D. 221 : AUG. A.D. 222 : DIED A.D. 235.

1. Obv. **IMP CAES M AVREL SEV ALEXANDER PIVS FELIX AVG**   Bust of Severus Alexander r., slightly bearded and laur., wearing paludamentum and cuirass : border of dots.

   Rev. **AEQVITAS AVGVSTI**   The three Monetæ, each holding scales and cornucopiæ, and having at her feet a conical heap of metal ; the outer Monetæ stand l., the centre one faces : border of dots.

   Æ 1·5.   Wt. 558·7 grs.   Pl. XXXVIII. fig. 3.

   This medallion has been gilt.

2. Obv. **IMP CAES M AVR SEV ALEXANDER AVG**   Bust of Severus Alexander r., laur., wearing paludamentum and cuirass : border of dots.

   Rev. **PONTIF MAX TR P II COS P P**   View of the Flavian Amphitheatre or Colosseum from above ; in each archway of the two middle storeys is a figure ; in the cornice are fixed the masts of the velarium ; within are the spectators ; to l. of building, the Emperor r., wearing pontifical robes and accompanied by an attendant ; on their l., a figure, holding rudder, and behind them, the Meta Sudans ; to r. of building, a porch, surmounted by pediment : border of dots.

   Æ 1·1.   Pl. XXXVIII. fig. 4.

3. Obv. Same inscription. Bust of Severus Alexander r., slightly bearded and laur., wearing paludamentum and cuirass : border of dots.

   Rev. **PONTI F MAX TR P V COS II P P** (In exergue) **LIB AVG III**   Emperor, laur., wearing toga and holding scroll in l. hand, seated l. on curule chair placed upon a suggestum, and presiding at a congiarium ; behind him, a præfect wearing toga, and a prætorian soldier armed with spear and shield ; before him, Liberalitas, wearing tunic and peplum, and holding tessera frumentaria and cornucopiæ ; a citizen is mounting the steps of the suggestum, and receiving in the folds of his dress gifts from the Emperor ; the suggestum is ornamented with four figures : border of dots.

   Æ 1·05.   Pl. XXXVIII. fig. 5.

4. Obv. IMP SEV ALE XANDER AVG Bust of Severus Alexander r., slightly bearded and laur., wearing paludamentum and cuirass: border of dots.

Rev. P M TR P VIIII (In exergue) COS III P P Emperor, laur. and wearing toga, seated l. on curule chair, holding on r. hand Victory with wreath, and with l. sceptre; he is crowned by Victory, who stands behind him, wearing tunic and peplum, and holding palm with l. hand; before him, Roma l., looking back, helmeted, and wearing short doubled tunic which leaves r. breast bare; she holds parazonium with l. hand, and supports with r. shield, placed upon a pillar, and inscribed [VIC]T / [AVG] : border of dots.

Æ 1·4. Pl. XXXVIII. fig. 6.

This medallion is struck in two metals.

5. Obv. Same inscription and border, and similar type.

Rev. PONTIF MAX TR P X COS III P P (In exergue) PROF AVG Emperor on horseback r., laur., wearing paludamentum and cuirass, and holding spear; horse walking; he is preceded by Victory, bearing wreath and palm, and wearing doubled tunic which leaves r. breast bare, and is followed by a prætorian soldier armed with spear; in the background behind the Emperor are two standards: border of dots. Æ 1·55. Pl. XXXIX. fig. 1.

6. Obv. Same inscription and border, and similar type.

Rev. FIDES MILI TVM Emperor r., laur., wearing paludamentum and cuirass, and holding patera and sceptro, sacrificing at a lighted tripod, and crowned by a prætorian soldier at whose feet is a shield: before him, on the other side of the tripod, Jupiter l., between two standards, his chlamys hanging on r. arm, holding thunderbolt and sceptre; at his feet, eagle. Æ 1·5.

This medallion is struck in two metals, the rim being of a lighter colour.

7. Obv. Same inscription. Bust of Severus Alexander r., laur., wearing paludamentum: border of dots.

Rev. Same inscription and similar type, but no eagle at the feet of Jupiter, and no standard before him: border of dots.

Æ 1. Pl. XXXIX. fig. 2.

8. *Obv.* **IMP CAES M AVREL SEV ALEX ANDER PIVS FELIX AVG** Bust of Severus Alexander r., slightly bearded and laur., wearing paludamentum and cuirass: border of dots.

Rev. **ROMAE AETERNAE** Emperor l., wearing pontifical robes, and holding patera and scroll, sacrificing at a garlanded and lighted altar, placed in front of a distyle temple of the Corinthian order, within which is a figure of Roma, seated, facing, holding spear; behind the Emperor are two attendants with palms, on the other side of the altar, two Flamines Diales r., wearing laenae and albogaleri, and behind them, Fortuna r., with rudder: the tympanum of the pediment of the temple is ornamented with a standing figure between two others recumbent; on the apex and on each of the angles of the pediment is an armed figure: border of dots.

Æ 1·55.   Pl. XXXIX. fig. 3.

9. *Obv.* **IMP ALEXAN DER PIVS AVG** Bust of Severus Alexander r., laur., wearing paludamentum: border of dots.

Rev. **SPES PVBLICA** Spes advancing l.; she holds up the skirt of her doubled tunic with l. hand, and with r. presents small Victory to the Emperor, who stands before her, clad in paludamentum and cuirass, and holding spear; he is accompanied by two soldiers, one of whom, in advance, holds purse and sceptre, and the other, behind, purse: border of dots.   Æ 1.   Pl. XXXIX. fig. 4.

SEVERUS ALEXANDER AND JULIA MAMAEA.

1. Obv. IMP SEV ALEXAND AVG IVLIA MAMAEA AVG (Below) MAT AVG
   Busts, face to face, of Severus Alexander r., laur., wearing paludamentum and cuirass, and Julia Mamæa l., draped and wearing stephane, her hair wavy: border of dots.

   Rev. FELICI TAS TEM PORVM   Emperor, togate, holding globe and scroll, seated l. on curule chair; he is crowned by Victory, with palm in l. hand, wearing tunic and peplum; before him, two female figures, one l., (Felicitas?) the other facing, head r., (Julia Mamæa?) leaning with r. hand on sceptre: border of dots.   Æ 1.   Pl. XL. fig. 1.

2. Obv. IMP SEV ALEXAND AVG IVLIA MAMAEA AVG   (Below)
   MATER AVG   Same type and border.

   Rev. [FE]LICI TAS TEMPORVM   Same type and border.   Æ 1·1.

3. Obv. IMP SEV ALEXANDER AVG IVLIA MAMAEA AVG   (Below)
   MATER AVG   Same type and border.

   Rev. FIDES MILI TVM   Emperor r., laur., wearing paludamentum and cuirass, and holding patera and sceptre, sacrificing at a lighted tripod, and crowned by a prætorian soldier, at whose feet is a shield: before him, on the other side of the tripod, Jupiter l., between two standards, his chlamys hanging on r. arm, holding thunderbolt and sceptre; at his feet, eagle: border of dots.   Æ 1·6.

   This medallion is struck in two metals.

4. Obv. IMP SEV ALEXAND AVG IVLIA MAMAEA AVG   (Below)
   MATER AVG   Same type and border.

   Rev. Same inscription.   Similar type, but no eagle at the feet of Jupiter and no signum in front of him: same border.   Æ 1·05.

5. Obv. Same.

   Rev. PONTIF MAX TR P X COS III P P (In exergue) PROF AVG   Emperor on horseback r., laur., wearing paludamentum and cuirass, and holding spear; horse walking; he is preceded by Victory, clad in doubled tunic which leaves r. breast bare, and carrying wreath and palm, and is followed by a prætorian soldier, armed with spear and shield; behind the Emperor, in the background, two standards: border of dots.   Æ 1·05.   Pl. XL. fig. 2.

JULIA MAMAEA.

Died a.d. 235.

1. Obv. **IVLIA MAMAEA AVGVSTA** Bust of Julia Mamæa r., wearing stephane ornamented with ears of corn, necklace, and tunic; she is winged, and behind her neck is a crescent; on r. arm she holds cornucopiæ, and with l. hand, portion of her dress, torch from which ears of corn are sprouting, and caduceus: border of dots.

    Rev. **FELICITAS PERPETVA** Julia Mamæa, wearing stephane tunic and peplum, seated l., her feet on footstool, holding sceptre with l. hand; she is accompanied by three female figures clad in the same manner, one of whom, in front, presents globe to her, another, Felicitas l., behind, holds caduceus, a third, in background to r. of the Empress, stands facing: border of dots.   Æ 1·45. Pl. XL. fig. 3.

    This medallion is struck in two metals.

2. Obv. Same.

    Rev. Same.   Æ 1·5.

    This medallion is struck in two metals, the rim being of a lighter colour.

3. Obv. Same inscription. Bust of Julia Mamæa l., wearing stephane and draped, hair wavy: border of dots.

    Rev. **MATER CASTRORVM** Julia Mamæa, wearing tunic and peplum, and holding patera and cornucopiæ, seated l. on throne; before her, an aquila and a signum; behind her, Securitas l., similarly clad, holding sceptre and leaning on low pillar, her l. leg crossed in front of the r.: border of dots.   Æ 1·05. Pl. XL. fig. 4.

4. Obv. Same.

    Rev. **TEMPORVM FELICITAS** Julia Mamæa, wearing tunic and peplum, and holding patera and sceptre, seated l. on throne; before her, a garlanded altar and a female figure l., similarly clad, extending r. hand and holding sceptre with l.; behind her, Felicitas l., her dress the same, holding with l. hand long caduceus: border of dots.

    Æ 1·05.

MAXIMIN I.

(MAXIMINVS, GERMANICVS.)

Aug. a.d. 235: Died a.d. 238.

Obv. IMP MAXIMINVS PIVS AVG Bust of Maximin r., laur. and slightly bearded, wearing paludamentum and cuirass: border of dots.

Rev. AEQVITAS AVGVSTI The three Monetæ l., each holding scales and cornucopiæ, and having at her feet a conical heap of metal: border of dots.   Ӕ 1·25. Wt. 333·7 **grs.** Pl. XL. fig. 5.

PUPIENUS.

(MARCVS CLODIVS PVPIENVS MAXIMVS.)

Aug. a.d. 238: Died a.d. 238.

Obv. IMP CAES M CLOD PVPIENVS AVG Bust of Pupienus l., bearded and laur., wearing paludamentum and cuirass ornamented with head of Medusa, and holding on r. hand globe surmounted by Victory r. bearing wreath, and with l. parazonium: border of dots.

Rev. LIBERALITAS AVGVSTORVM Balbinus Pupienus and Gordian III., togate, seated l. on curule chairs placed upon a suggestum, presiding at a congiarium; behind them, a prætorian soldier armed with spear; before them, Liberalitas l., wearing tunic and peplum, and holding tessera frumentaria and cornucopiæ; a citizen is mounting the steps of the suggestum and extending his hands to receive gifts: border of dots.   Æ 1·6.

This medallion is struck in two metals, the rim being of a lighter colour.

GORDIAN III.

(MARCVS ANTONIVS GORDIANVS.)

Caes. a.d. 238 : Aug. a.d. 238 : Died a.d. 244.

1. **Obv.** IMP GORDIANVS PIVS FEL AVG   Bust of Gordian r., laur., wearing paludamentum and cuirass.

    Rev. AEQVITAS AVGVSTI   The three Monotæ l., each holding scales and cornucopiæ, and having at her feet a conical heap of metal.

Æ 1·2.   Wt. 316·9 grs.

2. **Obv.** IMP GORDIANVS PIVS FELIX AVG   Bust of Gordian l., laur. and slightly bearded, wearing paludamentum and cuirass, and holding spear ? with r. hand : the cuirass is ornamented with a relief representing the Emperor on horseback l., hurling spear at a barbarian ; before him, Victory with wreath and palm, behind him, prostrate barbarian : border of dots.

    Rev. VIRTVS AVGVSTI   Emperor l., laur., wearing paludamentum and cuirass, holding in l. hand reversed spear, and with r. receiving globe from Sol r., radiate, standing before him, wearing chlamys and holding whip in l. hand ; between them, a soldier, facing, and at their feet, two captives seated face to face ; the Emperor is crowned by Roma l., helmeted, clad in short doubled tunic which leaves r. breast bare, and resting l. hand on shield ; behind Sol, a soldier with spear and vexillum, and, in the background, three signa : border of dots.   Æ 1·4.   Wt. 447·9 grs.   Pl. XLI. fig. 1.

    This medallion has been gilt.

3. **Obv.** IMP GORDIANVS PIVS FELIX AVG   Bust of Gordian r., laur., wearing paludamentum and cuirass ornamented with head of Medusa, and holding spear ? with l. hand : border of dots.

    Rev. PONTIFEX MAX TR P IIII   (In exergue) COS II PP   Triumphal quadriga, facing, in which is the Emperor l., holding laurel-branch with r. hand and sceptre with l., accompanied by Victory l., who crowns him with wreath and holds palm ; two of the horses are turned to r. and two to l., the outer ones being conducted by Mars and Roma, each carrying spear : border of dots.   Æ 1·45.   Pl. XLI. fig. 2.

    This medallion is struck in two metals, the rim being of a lighter colour.

4. Obv. IMP GORDIANVS PIVS FEL AVG Bust of Gordian r., laur., wearing paludamentum and cuirass: border of dots.

Rev. Same inscription. Emperor in triumphal quadriga l.; he holds laurel-branch with r. hand, and sceptre surmounted by eagle with l., and is accompanied by Victory, who crowns him with wreath, and holds palm; the horses are conducted by Roma, who looks back; she wears doubled tunic which leaves r. breast bare, and carries spear in r. hand; in the background, the head of a soldier is seen between two palms: border of dots. Æ 1·1. Pl. XLI. fig. 3.

5. Obv. IMP GORDIANVS PIVS FELIX AVG Bust of Gordian l., laur., wearing paludamentum and cuirass, and holding spear ? with r. hand; the cuirass is ornamented with a relief representing the Emperor on horseback l., and, behind him, a prostrate barbarian: border of dots.

Rev. PM TR P VII COS II P P View of the interior of the Circus Maximus: in the centre of the spina is an obelisk, and at each extremity three metæ: before the spina are five groups; the first represents a combat between two gladiators; the second, two wrestlers; the third, a pair of pancratiastæ; the fourth, two pugiles boxing with cæstus; and the fifth, a wounded gladiator being led away by an attendant; beyond the spina a race is taking place between two quadrigæ l., and further in the background is the Emperor in triumphal chariot drawn by six horses, and accompanied by Victory crowning him and holding palm; the chariot is preceded by three prætorian soldiers carrying long palms: border of dots. Æ 1·5. Pl. XLI. fig. 4.

This medallion is struck in two metals.

6. Obv. IMP C AES M ANT GORDIANVS AVG Bust of Gordian r., laur., wearing paludamentum and cuirass ornamented with head of Medusa, and holding spear ? with l. hand: border of dots.

Rev. ADLOCVTIO AVGVSTI Emperor, laur., and wearing paludamentum and cuirass, and accompanied by a præfect, standing l. on a suggestum, and addressing two auxiliaries ? l., and two legionaries r.: the former appear to be unarmed; of the latter, one holds shield, and the other, on whose l. is a horse, shield and spear; in the background are three spears and three standards, vexillum, signum, and aquila: border of dots. Æ 1·5. Pl. XLI. fig. 5.

This medallion is struck in two metals.

7. Obv. IMP CAES M ANT GORDIANVS AVG Bust of Gordian l., laur., wearing paludamentum and cuirass, and holding on r. hand globe surmounted by Victory r. bearing wreath: border of dots.

Rev. Same inscription and border, and similar type. Æ 1·4.

This medallion is struck in two metals.

GORDIAN III. 47

8. Obv. IMP GORDIANVS PIVS FELIX AVG Bust of Gordian r., laur., wearing cuirass and ægis on l. shoulder: the cuirass is ornamented with a relief representing the Emperor on horse **galloping** r.; beneath the horse, two prostrate barbarians: border of dots.

   Rev. Same inscription **and border, and similar type** r.: the auxiliaries? stand l., and, in the background, one spear only is seen.

   Æ 1·5. Pl. XLI. fig. 6.

   This medallion is struck in two metals.

9. Obv. Same inscription. Bust of Gordian l., laur., wearing paludamentum and cuirass: border of dots.

   Rev. **Same inscription** and border, and similar type. Æ 1·55.

   This medallion is struck in two metals, the rim being of a lighter colour.

10. Obv. IMP GORDIANVS PIVS FELIX AVG Bust of Gordian l., laur., wearing paludamentum **and cuirass, and** holding spear? with **r.** hand: the cuirass is ornamented **with** a relief representing the Emperor on horse **galloping** l.: border of dots.

    Rev. AEQVITAS AVGVSTI The three Monetæ l., each holding scales and cornucopiæ, and having at her feet a conical heap of metal: border of dots. Æ 1·4.

11. Obv. IMP GORDIANVS PIVS FELIX AVG Bust of Gordian l., laur., wearing paludamentum, and armed with spear? and shield, the latter ornamented with a relief.

    Rev. [FI] DES EXERCITVS Emperor l., laur., wearing paludamentum and cuirass, and holding spear, grasping with his r. hand that **of a soldier** r.; between them, in **the** background, two signa and a laurel-branch; **at their feet,** two river-gods, the Tigris and the Euphrates, reclining r. and l. on their urns; the one on l. holds in each hand a reed; the other on r. holds in r. hand a reed, **with** which he inscribes a shield; the **Emperor** is crowned by Victory, who holds palm with l. hand. Æ 1·5.

    This medallion is struck in two metals, the rim being of a lighter colour.

12. Obv. Same inscription. Bust of Gordian r., laur., wearing paludamentum and cuirass.

    Rev. LIBERALITAS AVG VSTI II Emperor, togate, seated l. on curule chair placed upon a suggestum, and presiding at a congiarium; behind him, a præfect and a prætorian soldier, who leans with l. hand on spear; before him, Liberalitas l., holding tessera frumentaria and cornucopiæ; a citizen is mounting the steps of the suggestum, and extending his hands to receive gifts; the base of the suggestum is ornamented with figures. Æ 1·45.

    This medallion is struck in two metals, the rim being of a lighter colour.

13. Obv. Same inscription. Bust of Gordian l., wearing paludamentum, and armed with spear? and shield, the latter ornamented with a relief representing the Emperor on horse galloping l., preceded by Victory bearing wreath, and followed by a soldier: border of dots.

Rev. MVNIFICENTIA GORDIANI AVG View of the Flavian Amphitheatro or Colosseum from above: within are three continuous rows of spectators, with the præfect of the games seated in their midst, witnessing a combat between a bull and an elephant with rider; in each archway of the two middle storeys is a figure, and within those of the lowermost, the inner archways are visible; in the cornice are fixed the masts of the velarium; on l., the Meta Sudans, and behind it, a male figure, facing, wearing wreath and holding rudder; on r., a porch surmounted by pediment, within which, a figure: border of dots. Æ 1·5. Pl. XLII. fig. 1.

14. Obv. IMP GORDIANVS PIVS FELIX AVG Bust of Gordian l., laur., wearing paludamentum and cuirass, and holding spear? with r. hand: the cuirass is ornamented with a relief representing the Emperor on horseback l., hurling spear at a barbarian; before him, Victory bearing wreath; behind him, a prostrate barbarian: border of dots.

Rev. P A X AETERNA Emperor l., wearing paludamentum and cuirass; he holds patera and spear, and sacrifices at a lighted altar; behind him, Victory l., crowning him with wreath and holding palm; before him, in the background, Sol in quadriga, facing, holding whip; two of the horses are turned to r. and two to l.; beneath the chariot are two river-gods, the Tigris and the Euphrates, reclining r. and l. on urns: on l., a signum; in the centre, behind Sol, a second; and a third, behind the Emperor: border of dots. Æ 1·6.

This medallion is struck in two metals, the rim being of a lighter colour.

15. Obv. Same as no. 13.

Rev. TRAIECTVS AVG Trireme r., in which are seen six rowers, four soldiers, and a pilot, (Emperor?) who is seated at the stern beneath an aplustre in the form of an elephant's head; one of the soldiers stands r. with foot on prow, and is armed with spear and shield; the other three l., hold respectively an aquila, a signum, and a vexillum; beneath the trireme, waves and dolphins: border of dots. Æ 1·55. Pl. XLII. fig. 2.

This medallion is struck in two metals, the rim being of a lighter colour.

16. **Obv.** Same inscription. **Bust** of Gordian l., laur., wearing paludamentum and cuirass: border of dots.

Rev. VICTO RIA AVG Circular temple of the Doric order with a tetrastyle portico, above the pediment of which **rises a dome; within** the tympanum is the inscription NEIKH, and **on the frieze,**
ΟΠΛ[ΟΦ]ΟΡΟC
Within is seen a standing statue of armed Victory: on **r.** of temple, Emperor l., wearing pontifical robes and holding patera, sacrificing at a lighted altar; behind him, two attendants, holding aloft palms: **on** l. **of** temple, a popa, with axe raised, slaying an ox, behind which **is** a victimarius: border of dots. Æ 1·65. Pl. XLII. fig. 3.

This medallion is struck in two metals.

17. **Obv.** Same inscription. Bust of Gordian r., **laur.**, wearing paludamentum and cuirass: border of dots.

Rev. VIR TVS AVGV STI Emperor seated l., on cuirass, holding sceptre **with l. hand, and** extending **r.** towards two soldiers standing before him, **one of whom holds** signum and parazonium, the other, signum and shield; **between** them and **the** Emperor a figure, facing; the **Emperor is crowned** by Victory, **who** stands behind him, wearing **doubled** tunic and holding palm with l. **hand; at her feet,** a helmet and two shields: border of dots. Æ 1·5.

This medallion is struck in two metals, the rim being of a lighter colour.

PHILIP I.

(MARCVS IVLIVS PHILIPPVS, GERMANICVS MAXIMVS, CARPICVS MAXIMVS.)

AUG. A.D. 244: DIED A.D. 249.

Obv. IMP CAES M IVL PHILIPPVS AVG Bust of Philip r., laur., wearing paludamentum and cuirass: border of dots.

Rev. [VIRTV]S AVGVSTI Jupiter r., leaning with l. hand on sceptre, and presenting with r. globe to the Emperor, who stands l., wearing paludamentum and cuirass, and holding sceptre with l. hand; between them, an aquila; the Emperor is crowned by a prætorian soldier, who stands behind him, armed with parazonium, and resting l. hand on shield; behind Jupiter, Virtus r., helmeted, wearing short doubled tunic which leaves r. breast bare, and holding spear.   Æ 1·3.

OTACILIA.

(MARCIA OTACILIA SEVERA.)

1. Obv. **MARCIA OTACIL SEVERA AVG** Bust of Otacilia l., draped and wearing stephano; her hair wavy and with a plait at the back of the head: border of dots.

   Rev. **PVDICITIA AVG** Otacilia as Pudicitia, seated l., wearing **tunic and** poplum; with **r.** hand she draws veil over her face, and holds sceptre with l.; before her, two children r., and behind her, Felicitas l., wearing tunic and poplum, and holding caduceus and cornucopiæ: border of dots. Æ 1·45. Pl. XLIII. fig. 1.

2. Same. Æ 1·55.

   This medallion is struck in two metals.

PHILIP I. AND PHILIP II.

Obv. **CONCORDIA AVGVSTORVM** Busts, face to face, of Philip I. r., and Philip II. l., each laur., and wearing paludamentum and cuirass: border of dots.

Rev. **AD VENTVS AV G G** The two Emperors on horseback l.: each raises his r. hand, and the nearer horseman holds sceptre with l.; they are preceded by Victory, wearing doubled tunic, and carrying wreath and palm, and are followed by two prætorian soldiers, one of whom carries spear, the other, shield; in the background are seen two soldiers, a vexillum, an aquila, and a signum: border of dots.
Æ 1·5.   Pl. XLIII. fig. 2.

This medallion is struck in two metals, the rim being of a lighter colour.

PHILIP I., OTACILIA, AND PHILIP II.

1. Obv. **CONCORDIA AVGVSTORVM** Busts jugate, r., of Philip I., laur., wearing paludamentum and cuirass, and Otacilia, draped and wearing stephane; facing them, the bust of Philip II. l., bare-headed, wearing paludamentum and cuirass: border of dots.

    Rev. **P M T R PIIICOS PP** The two Emperors facing each other, togate, and holding paterae, sacrificing at a lighted altar placed in front of a temple, surmounted by eight small porticoes, four of which have within them standing figures; each Emperor is accompanied by an attendant holding spear? border of dots.
    Æ 1·55. Pl. XLIII. fig. 3.

    This medallion is struck in two metals, the rim being of a lighter colour.

2. Obv. Same.

    Rev. **P ONTIFEX MAX TR P IIII** (In exergue) **COS II P P** The two Emperors l., in triumphal quadriga, facing; Philip I. holds laurel-branch in r. hand, and is crowned by Victory, who holds palm with l. hand; Philip II. extends his r. hand; two of the horses are turned to l., and two to r.; those to l. are conducted by Roma, helmeted, and wearing short doubled tunic which leaves r. breast bare, carrying spear and palm; those to r., by Mars, helmeted, and wearing chlamys and cuirass, carrying with r. hand palm, and with l. spear and shield: border of dots. Æ 1·65. Pl. XLIV. fig. 1.

    This medallion is struck in two metals, the rim being of a lighter colour.

3. Obv. Same.

    Rev. **EX ORACVLO APOLLINIS** Circular temple with colonnade raised upon a lofty stylobate; a narrow flight of steps leads up to the peristyle, of which four columns are seen; in the centre intercolumniation is a doorway, disclosing a seated statue of Jupiter; the entablature, which is equal in height to the stylobate, consists of an architrave, frieze, and cornice, the last being surmounted by an enriched open fretwork; a dome crowns the whole, and is surmounted by an eagle seated on a globo: border of dots.
    Æ 1·65. Pl. XLIV. fig. 2.

    This medallion is struck in two metals, the rim being of a lighter colour.

4. *Obv.* Same inscription and similar type; the bust of Philip II. laur.: border of dots.

   Rev. **SAECVLVM NOVVM** The two Emperors facing each other, wearing pontifical robes and holding pateræ, sacrificing at a garlanded altar, placed in front of an octostyle temple; each is accompanied by two attendants; between the altar and the temple, a tibicen, facing, playing a double flute; the tympanum of the pediment of the temple is ornamented with a standing figure between two others recumbent; on each of the lower angles of the pediment is a Victory, and on the apex, a group of three figures: border of dots.

   Æ 1·6. Pl. XLIV. fig. 3.

OTACILIA, PHILIP I., AND PHILIP II.

1. Obv. MARCIA OTACIL SEVERA AVG Bust of Otacilia r., draped, and wearing stephane; her hair wavy and with a plait at the back of the head : border of dots.

    Rev. PIETAS AVGVSTORVM (Beneath) III ET II COS Busts, face to face, of Philip I. r., bearded, and Philip II. l., each laur., and wearing paludamentum and cuirass: border of dots.
    Æ 1·6.   Pl. XLV. fig. 1.

    This medallion is struck in two metals, the rim being of a lighter colour.

2. Same. Æ 1·55.

    This medallion is struck in two metals, and is gilt.

PHILIP II.

Caes. a.d. 244 : Aug. a.d. 247 : Died a.d. 249.

Obv. M IVL PHILIPPVS NOBIL CAES Youthful bust of Philip r., bareheaded, wearing tunic and paludamentum : border of dots.

Rev. PRINCIPI IVVEN TVTIS Cæsar, wearing paludamentum and cuirass, and holding globe and reversed spear, standing l. between Roma on his r., and Mars on his l. : Roma is helmeted, and wears short doubled tunic which leaves r. breast bare ; she rests her r. hand on shield, and holds signum in l. ; Mars, helmeted, and wearing chlamys and cuirass, crowns Philip with r. hand, and holds with l. signum and shield : border of dots.   Æ 1·5. Pl. XLV. fig. 2.

This medallion is struck in two metals, the rim being of a lighter colour.

GALLUS.

(CAIVS VIBIVS TREBONIANVS GALLVS.)

Aug. A.D. 251: Died A.D. 254.

1. Obv. IMP CAES C VIBIVS TREBONIANVS GALLVS AVG   Bust of Gallus r., bearded and laur., wearing paludamentum and cuirass: border of dots.

    Rev. IVNONI M ARTIALI   Circular monopteral temple of Corinthian style, within which is a statue of Juno seated on a throne, holding ears of corn in r. hand and globe on extended l.; the temple has a circle of columns surmounted by a dome; the frieze is ornamented with a series of wreaths; the outer face of the dome is ribbed, and garlands are hung within it; the inner columns are represented in perspective; on either side of Juno, against the bases of each of the further columns, are two objects like gorgon's heads: border of dots. Æ 1·2. Wt. 350·2 grs. Pl. XLV. fig. 3.

    This medallion has been gilt.

2. Obv. Same inscription and similar type; the paludamentum being edged on l. shoulder with fringe: border of dots.

    Rev. MONETA A VGG   The three Monetæ l., each holding scales and cornucopiæ, and having at her feet a conical heap of metal: border of dots. Æ 1·35. Wt. 449·3 grs.

    This medallion has been gilt.

3. Obv. Same inscription and border, and similar type.

    Rev. MONETA AV GG   Same type and border.
    Æ 1·25. Wt. 313·7 grs. Pl. XLVI. fig. 1.

    This medallion has been gilt.

4. Obv. IMP CAE C VIB TREB GALLVS AVG   Bust of Gallus r., bearded and radiate, wearing paludamentum and cuirass: border of dots.

    Rev. ARN AZI   Apollo, laur., standing l. on a mountain, holding laurel-branch with r. hand and serpent with l.: border of dots. Æ 1.

5. *Obv.* IMP CAES C VIBIVS TREBONIANVS GALLVS AVG   Bust of Gallus r., bearded and laur., wearing cuirass and paludamentum edged on l. shoulder with fringe : border of dots.

Rev. Same inscription and similar type to no. 1, with the following chief exceptions: the l. hand of Juno is not extended and does not hold globe; on l. of throne, which apparently has wings, is a peacock; under the dome hangs a massive pendent; the objects resembling gorgons' heads are seen between the columns, and are mounted on pedestals: border of dots.   Æ 1·55.   Pl. XLVI. fig. 2.

This medallion is struck in two metals, the rim being of a lighter colour.

GALLUS AND VOLUSIAN.

1. Obv. IMP GALLVS AVG IMP VOLVSIANVS AVG   Busts, face to face, of Gallus r. and Volusian l., each laur., and wearing paludamentum and cuirass : border of dots.

   Rev. FORTVNA E R ED VCI   The two Emperors, wearing pontifical robes and holding pateræ, standing facing each other, and sacrificing at a garlanded and lighted altar placed in front of a hexastyle temple of the Corinthian order : the Emperor on the r. is crowned by a senator l., holding staff with l. hand; behind, a soldier carrying spear ; behind the Emperor on the l., at whose feet is a bull, are two soldiers r., one of whom, helmeted, crowns the Emperor, the other leans with r. hand on spear ; between the temple and the altar, a tibicen l., playing double flute : within the temple is seen a seated statue of Fortuna, holding rudder and cornucopiæ ; the tympanum of the pediment is ornamented with a wreath ; on the l. angle of the pediment, Fortuna holding rudder and cornucopiæ, and on the r., statue with shield and spear : border of dots.

   Æ 1·45.   Pl. XLVI. fig. 3.

   This medallion is struck in two metals, the rim being of a lighter colour.

2. Obv. Same.

   Rev. IVNONIM ARTIALI   Type similar to medallion no. 5 of Gallus : border of dots.   Æ 1·5.

VOLUSIAN.

(CAIVS VIBIVS AFINIVS GALLVS VINDVMINVS VOLVSIANVS.)

CAES. A.D. 251 : AUG. A.D. 252 : DIED A.D. 254.

1. Obv. **IMP CAE C VIB VOLVSIANO AVG** Bust of Volusian r., bearded and laur., wearing cuirass and paludamentum edged on l. shoulder with fringe: border of dots.

    Rev. **MONETA A VGG** The three Monetæ l., each holding scales and cornucopiæ, and having at her feet a conical heap of metal: border of dots. Æ 1·2. Wt. 373·3 grs. Pl. XLVII. fig. 1.

    This medallion has been gilt.

2. Obv. Same inscription and border, and similar type.

    Rev. **AD VENTVS AVGG** Gallus and Volusian on horseback l.; the nearer wears paludamentum and cuirass; both raise r. hands; they are preceded by Victory, wearing doubled tunic, and carrying wreath and palm, and are followed by a prætorian soldier, carrying shield; in the background, a vexillum and two signa: border of dots. Æ 1·45.

3. Obv. **IMP CAE C VIB V OLVSIANO AVG** Bust of Volusian l., laur., wearing tunica palmata and toga picta, and holding in r. hand sceptro surmounted by eagle: border of dots.

    Rev. **VIRTVS AVGVSTORVM** Emperor l., wearing paludamentum and cuirass, and holding patera and reversed spear, sacrificing at a lighted tripod; before him, on l. of tripod, a bull with l. knee bent, and a tibicen r., playing double flute; behind the Emperor, a prætorian soldier, who crowns him, resting l. hand on shield; in the background, an aquila and a signum: border of dots. Æ 1·5.

    This medallion is struck in two metals, the rim being of a lighter colour.

4. Obv. **IMP CAE C VIB VOLVSIANO AVG** Bust of Volusian r., bearded and laur., wearing paludamentum and cuirass : border of dots.

    Rev. **ARN AZI** Apollo, laur., standing l. on a mountain, holding laurel-branch with r. hand and serpent with l.: border of dots. Æ 1·25.

VALERIAN.

(CAIVS PVBLIVS LICINIVS VALERIANVS, GERMANICVS MAXIMVS.)

Aug. a.d. 253: Capt. a.d. 260.

1. Obv. IMP CAES P LIC VALERIANVS AVG   Bust of Valerian l., laur., wearing paludamentum and cuirass: border of dots.
   Rev. MONETA AVGG   The three Monetæ l., each holding scales and cornucopiæ, and having at her feet a conical heap of metal: border of dots.   Æ 1·35. Wt. 420·8 grs.
   This medallion has been gilt.

2. Obv. IMP C PLIC VALERIANVS P F AVG   Bust of Valerian r., laur., wearing paludamentum and cuirass: border of dots.
   Rev. MO NETAE AV GG   Same type and border.
   Æ 1·3. Wt. 409·3 grs.

3. Obv. IMP CAES P LIC VALERIANVS AVG   Bust of Valerian l., laur., wearing paludamentum and cuirass: border of dots.
   Rev. L IB ERALITAS AVGG I   Valerian and Gallienus, laur. and togato, seated l. on curule chairs placed upon a suggestum, and presiding at a congiarium; each holds scroll in l. hand, and is accompanied by a præfect, who stands behind him; before them, Liberalitas l., wearing tunic and peplum, and holding tessera frumentaria and cornucopiæ; a citizen is mounting the steps of the suggestum, and receiving gifts in the folds of his cloak: border of dots.
   Æ 1·5. Pl. XLVII. fig. 2.
   This medallion is struck in two metals, the rim being of a lighter colour.

4. Obv. IMP C PLIC VALERIANVS P F AVG   Bust of Valerian r., laur., wearing cuirass and paludamentum edged on l. shoulder with fringe: border of dots.
   Rev. VICTO RIA AVGVSTORVM   Valerian and Gallienus, each laur. and wearing paludamentum and cuirass, standing face to face, and supporting on their r. hands globe surmounted by Victory holding open wreath with both hands; each Emperor holds reversed spear with l. hand, and is accompanied by a soldier, the one on r. holding vexillum and shield, the other on l., spear and signum: border of dots.   Æ 1·5. Pl. XLVII. fig. 3.
   This medallion is struck in two metals.

VALERIAN, VALERIAN THE YOUNGER, GALLIENUS, AND SALONINA.

Obv. **PIETAS AVGVSTORVM** Busts, face to face, of Valerian l., laur., wearing cuirass, and of Valerian the Younger r., bare-headed, wearing paludamentum and cuirass: border of dots.

Rev. **CONCORDIA AVGVSTORVM** Busts, face to face, of Gallienus l., bearded and laur., wearing cuirass, and of Salonina r., wearing stephane and draped; her hair is wavy and with a plait at the back of the head: border of dots.

$\mathcal{R}$ 1·35.   Wt. 423·7 grs.   Pl. XLVII. fig. 4.

VALERIAN AND GALLIENUS.

Obv. **CONCORDIA AVGVSTORVM** Busts, face to face, of Valerian l., laur., wearing paludamentum and cuirass, and of Gallienus r., bearded and laur., wearing cuirass: border of dots.

Rev. **LIBER ALITAS AVGG** The two Emperors, laur. and togate, seated l. on curule chairs placed upon a suggestum, and presiding at a congiarium; each holds scroll in l. hand, and is accompanied by a prefect, who stands behind him; before them, Liberalitas l., wearing tunic and peplum, and holding tessera frumentaria and cornucopiæ; a citizen is mounting the steps of the suggestum, and receiving gifts in the folds of his cloak: border of dots. Æ ·9.

GALLIENUS.

(PVBLIVS LICINIVS GALLIENVS, GERMANICVS MAXIMVS.)

Aug. a.d. 253 : Died a.d. 268.

1. Obv. **IMP GALLIENVS AVG COS V** Bust of Gallienus r., bearded and laur.: border of dots.

   Rev. **MONETA A VG** The three Monetæ l., each holding scales and cornucopiæ, and having at her feet a conical heap of metal: border of dots.   N 1·25. Wt. 357·7 grs. Pl. XLVIII. fig. 1.

2. Obv. **GALLIE NO PIO AVG** Bust of Gallienus l., laur., wearing paludamentum: border of dots.

   Rev. **P A X A V G** In field, **S C** Pax l., wearing tunic and peplum, and holding olive-branch and sceptre: border of dots.   N 1·2. Wt. 471·3 grs.

   This gold piece, the reverse of which is in all probability struck from a large brass die, may have been a pattern.

3. Obv. **IMP GALLIENVS AVG** Bust of Gallienus l., bearded, wearing crested helmet and cuirass, and armed with spear and shield, the latter being ornamented with head of Medusa; over r. shoulder is the parazonium-strap: border of dots.

   Rev. **VIRTVS AVG** Hercules towards r., wearing wreath; he rests r. hand on club, and holds with l. strung bow and lion's skin: border of dots.   N 1·05. Wt. 204·6 grs. Pl. XLVIII. fig. 2.

4. Obv. **IMP GALLIENVS PIVS FELIX AVG** Bust of Gallienus r., bearded and laur., wearing paludamentum and cuirass.

   Rev. **FIDES MIL [ITVM]** Fides l., wearing tunic and peplum, and holding signum with each hand: border of dots.   Æ ·9.

5. Obv. **[GALLIENVS PIVS FEL AVG]** Head of Gallienus r., bearded, wearing lion's skin: border of dots.

   Rev. **M ONETA A V G** The three Monetæ l., each holding scales and cornucopiæ, and having at her feet a conical heap of metal: border of dots.   Æ 1·7. Pl. XLVIII. fig. 3.

   The inscription of the obv. of this medallion has been effaced.

6. Obv. IMP GALLIENVS PIVS FEL AVG Bust of Gallienus r., bearded and laur., wearing paludamentum and cuirass: border of dots.

   Rev. MONETA AVG Same type and border. Æ 1·35.

7. Obv. IMP GALLIENVS P F AVG Bust of Gallienus r., bearded and laur., wearing paludamentum and cuirass ornamented with head of Medusa, and holding with l. hand spear: border of dots.

   Rev. MONETA AVG Same type and border. Bil. 1·5.

8. Obv. IMP GALLIENVS P F AVG Bust of Gallienus l., bearded and laur., wearing cuirass, and armed with spear and shield; over r. shoulder is the parazonium-strap; the cuirass and shield are each ornamented with head of Medusa: border of dots.

   Rev. MONETA AVGG Same type and border. Æ 1·4.

   This medallion has been gilt.

9. Obv. IMP GALLIENVS P F AVG Bust of Gallienus r., bearded and laur., wearing cuirass.

   Rev. MONETA A VGG Same type and border. Bil. 1·1.

   This medallion has been gilt.

10. Obv. G ALLIENVM AVG P R Bust of Gallienus l., bearded and laur., wearing paludamentum and cuirass, and armed with spear and shield: border of dots.

    Rev. OB CONSERVATIONEM SALVTIS Salus r., wearing stephane tunic and peplum, and holding with r. hand serpent, which she feeds from patera resting on her l.: border of dots.

    Bil. ·95. Pl. XLVIII. fig. 4.

11. Obv. GALLIENVM AVG SENATVS Bust of Gallienus l., bearded and laur., wearing tunic and toga picta: border of dots.

    Rev. OB LIBERTATEM RECEPTAM Libertas l., wearing stephane tunic and peplum, and holding cap and sceptre: border of dots. Bil. 1·05.

12. Obv. IMP GALLIENVS P F AVG Bust of Gallienus r., bearded and laur.: border of dots.

    Rev. P A X A V G Pax, wearing tunic and peplum, seated l. on throne; she holds olive-branch with r. hand, and sceptre with l.: border of dots. Bil. 1·4.

13. Obv. **IMP GALLIENVS P F AVG** Bust of Gallienus l., bearded and laur., wearing cuirass, and armed with spear and shield; over r. shoulder is the parazonium-strap; the shield is ornamented with head of Medusa: border of dots.

Rev. **VIRT VS A V G** Emperor, crowned by Victory, facing, looking l.; she holds palm in her l. hand; he stands r. and looks back as he places his r. hand on a trophy; with l. he holds shield against which rests spear; the shield is placed on a low rock; in front of the trophy is a captive, kneeling l. on r. knee, between two other captives, seated, their hands tied behind them: border of dots.

Æ 1·5.   Pl. XLVIII. fig. 5.

This medallion is struck in two metals, the rim being of a lighter colour.

14. Obv. **IMP C P LIC GALLIENVS AVG** Bust of Gallienus r., bearded and laur., wearing paludamentum and cuirass.

Rev. **VOTIS** within laurel-wreath.
DECENNA
LIBVS

Æ ·9.

GALLIENUS AND SALONINA.

1. Obv. **IMP GALLIENVS P F AVG** Bust of Gallienus l., bearded and laur., wearing cuirass, and armed with spear and shield; over r. shoulder is the parazonium-strap; the cuirass and the shield are each ornamented with head of Medusa: border of dots.

    Rev. **CORNELIA SALONINA AVGVSTA** Bust of Salonina r., wearing stephane, and draped; her hair wavy and with a plait at the back of the head: border of dots. Æ 1·4. Pl. XLIX. fig. 1.

2. Same. Æ 1·6.

3. Obv. **CONCORDIA AVGVSTORVM** Busts, face to face, of Gallienus r., bearded and laur., wearing cuirass and paludamentum edged on l. shoulder with fringe, and of Salonina l., wearing stephane, and draped; her hair wavy and with a plait at the back of the head.

    Rev. **AD VENTVS AV GG** Gallienus and Saloninus, laur., on horseback l.; their r. hands raised; the nearer horseman holds sceptre with l.; they are preceded by Victory, wearing doubled tunic, and carrying wreath and palm, and they are followed by a prætorian soldier, armed with spear and shield; in the background, a vexillum and a signum.
    Æ ·9.

4. Obv. **CONCORDIA AVGG** Similar type: border of dots.

    Rev. **AEQVITAS PVBLICA** The three Monetæ l., each holding scales and cornucopiæ, and having at her feet a conical heap of metal: border of dots. Æ 1·5. Pl. XLIX. fig. 2.

GALLIENUS AND SALONINUS.

Obv. **CONCORDIA AVGVSTORVM** Busts, face to face, of Gallienus l., bearded and laur., wearing cuirass, and of Saloninus r., bare-headed, and wearing paludamentum: border of dots.

Rev. **AD VEN TV SA VGG** The two Emperors, laur., on horseback l.; their r. hands raised; the nearer horseman (Gallienus) holds sceptre with l. hand; they are preceded by Victory, wearing doubled tunic, and carrying wreath and palm, and a figure, looking back, and they are followed by two prætorian soldiers, the hindermost of whom carries spear and shield; in the background, a vexillum an aquila and a signum: border of dots. Æ 1·55. Pl. L. fig. 1.

This medallion is struck in two metals, the rim being of a lighter colour.

SALONINA.

(CORNELIA SALONINA.)

1. Obv. **CORNELIA SALONINA AVGVSTA** Bust of Salonina r., wearing stephane, and draped; her hair wavy and with a plait at the back of the head: **border of dots**.

   Rev. **AEQVITAS PVBLICA** The three Monetæ l., each holding scales and cornucopiæ, and having at her feet a conical heap of metal: **border of dots**. Bil. 1·35. Pl. L. fig. 2.

2. Obv. **CORNELIA SALONINA AVG** Similar type, bust larger.
   Rev. **Same.** Bil. 1·4.

   This medallion has been gilt.

3. Obv. **CORN SALONINA AVG** Similar type to no. 1.

   Rev. **PVDICITIA AVG** Salonina, as Pudicitia, wearing tunic and peplum, seated l. on throne; with r. hand she draws her veil over her face, and holds sceptre with l. Bil. 1·1. Pl. L. fig. 3.

SALONINUS.

(PVBLIVS LICINIVS CORNELIVS SALONINVS VALERIANVS.)

Caes. a.d. 253 : Aug. a.d. 257 : Died a.d. 260.

1. Obv. LIC COR SAL VALERIANVS N CAES   Youthful bust of Saloninus r., bare-headed, wearing paludamentum and cuirass : border of dots.

    Rev. PRINCIPI IV VENTVTIS   Cæsar l., wearing paludamentum and cuirass, and holding globe on r. hand and sceptre with l.; before him, at his feet, a captive, seated l., in an attitude of grief : border of dots.
    Æ 1·65.   Pl. LI. fig. 1.

2. Obv. Same inscription and border, and similar type.

    Rev. PRINCIPI IVV ENTVTIS   Similar type and same border.   Æ 1·5.

    This medallion is plated.

CLAUDIUS II.

(MARCVS AVRELIVS CLAVDIVS, GOTHICVS.)

Aug. a.d. 268 : Died a.d. 270.

1. Obv. IMP CAES CLAVDI VS PIVS FELIX AVG Bust of Claudius r., bearded and laur., wearing paludamentum and cuirass.

    Rev. P M TR P II COS P P Hercules r., in an attitude of repose, resting his r. hand on his hip, and leaning with l. arm on his club, which is placed on a rock, and is covered with the lion's skin. Æ 1·65.

    This medallion is struck in two metals.

2. Obv. IMP CAES CLAVDIVS PIVS FEL AVG Bust of Claudius r., bearded and laur., wearing paludamentum and cuirass : border of dots.

    Rev. MONETA AVG The three Monetæ l., each holding scales and cornucopiæ, and having at her feet a conical heap of metal.

    Æ 1·55. Pl. LI. fig. 2.

    This medallion has been gilt.

3. Obv. IMP C CLAVDIVS P F AVG Bust of Claudius r., bearded and laur., wearing paludamentum and cuirass : border of dots.

    Rev. M ONETA AVG Same type : border of dots.

    Æ 1·35. Pl. LI. fig. 3.

    This medallion has been gilt.

TACITUS.

(MARCVS CLAVDIVS TACITVS.)

Aug. a.d. 275 : Died a.d. 276.

Obv. **IMP C M CL TACITVS P F AVG** Bust of Tacitus r., laur., wearing paludamentum and cuirass.

Rev. **ADL OCVTIO AVG** Tacitus, wearing paludamentum and cuirass, standing l. on a suggestum and addressing two prætorian soldiers; he raises his r. hand, and holds spear with l.; behind him stands a præfect; the two soldiers are armed with spears and shields, and are accompanied by Victory, facing, holding palm.

Æ 1·1.   Pl. LII. fig. 1.

FLORIANUS.

(MARCVS ANNIVS FLORIANVS.)

Aug. a.d. 276: Died a.d. 276.

Obv. **IMP C M ANN FLORIANVS P AVG** Bust of Florianus r., **bearded** and laur., wearing paludamentum and cuirass: border of dots.

Rev. **MONETA AVG** The three Monetæ l., each holding scales and cornucopiæ, and having at her feet a conical heap of metal: border of dots. Æ 1·45. Pl. LII. fig. 2.

This medallion is plated.

PROBUS.

(MARCVS AVRELIVS PROBVS.)

Aug. a.d. 276: Died a.d. 282.

1. Obv. IMPCPROBVSI NVICPFAVG   Busts, jugate, r., of Probus, bearded and laur., wearing paludamentum and cuirass, and armed with spear and shield ornamented within, and of Sol, radiate: border of dots.

   Rev. M O N E T A A V G   The three Monetæ l., each holding scales and cornucopiæ, and having at her feet a conical heap of metal: border of dots.   Æ 1·5.   Pl. LIII. fig. 1.

   This medallion is plated, and shews traces of gilding.

2. Obv. IMPCPROB VSPFAVG   Bust of Probus l., bearded and laur., wearing paludamentum and cuirass ornamented with head of Medusa; he holds on r. hand globe surmounted by Victory r. with wreath, and with l. parazonium: border of dots.

   Rev. MONETAA VG   Same type and border.   Æ 1·55.   Pl. LIII. fig. 2.

   This medallion is plated, and shews traces of gilding.

3. Obv. IMPPROBV SPFAVG   Bust of Probus l., bearded and laur., wearing paludamentum and cuirass, and armed with spear and shield, the latter being ornamented with a relief representing the Emperor on horseback l., preceded by Victory carrying wreath and followed by a soldier armed with spear and shield: border of dots.

   Rev. M ONETAA VG   Same type and border.
   Æ 1·25.   Pl. LIII. fig. 3.

   This medallion is plated, and shews traces of gilding.

4. Obv. IMPPRO BVSPFAVG   Bust of Probus l., bearded and laur., wearing cuirass ornamented with head of Medusa; he holds with r. hand spear? and has on l. arm shield, as on previous medallion: border of dots.

   Rev. MO NETAA VG   Similar type, and same border.
   Æ 1·4.   Pl. LIII. fig. 4.

   This medallion shews traces of plating and gilding.

5. Obv. IMPPROB VSPFAVG   Bust of Probus l., bearded and laur., wearing paludamentum and cuirass: border of dots.

   Rev. MO NETAAV G   Same type and border.   Æ 1·3.

   This medallion has been gilt.

6. Obv. **IMP PROB VS AVG** Bust of Probus r., bearded and laur., wearing cuirass ornamented with head of Medusa; from l. shoulder hangs the ægis; **with l.** hand he holds parazonium : **border of dots.**

Rev. **MONETA AVG** Similar type, and same border. Æ 1·5.

This medallion has been gilt.

7. Obv. **PROBVS IN VICT P AVG** Bust of **Probus** l., bearded and laur., **holding spear with** r. hand, and wearing **on l.** shoulder ægis : border of dots.

Rev. **MO NETA AV G** Similar type, and same border.

Æ 1·5. Pl. LIII. fig. 5.

This medallion is plated.

CARUS.

(MARCVS AVRELIVS CARVS.)

Aug. a.d. 282: Died a.d. 283.

Obv. **IMP C M AVR CARVS P F AVG** Bust of Carus r., laur., wearing paludamentum and cuirass: border of dots.

Rev. **MO NETA A VGG** The three Monetæ l., each holding scales and cornucopiæ, and having at her feet a conical heap of metal: border of dots. Æ 1·35. Pl. LIV. fig. 1.

This medallion has been plated.

NUMERIAN.

(MARCVS AVRELIVS NVMERIANVS.)

CAES. A.D. 282: AUG. A.D. 283: DIED A.D. 284.

1. Obv. IMP C NVMERIANVS P F AVG COS   Bust of Numerian r., laur., wearing tunica palmata and toga picta, holding with r. hand sceptre surmounted by eagle, and, on l. globe surmounted by Victory l. with wreath and palm: border of dots.

   Rev. ADLOCVTIO AVGG   Numerian and Carinus, each wearing paludamentum and cuirass, and raising his r. hand, standing l. on a suggestum, and addressing four soldiers r., the first of whom holds a spear; in the background are three standards, a signum a vexillum and an aquila; behind the Emperors, a præfect l.: border of dots.
   Æ 1·6.   Pl. LIV. fig. 4.

   This medallion is struck in two metals, and has been gilt.

2. Obv. IMP C NVMERIANVS P F AVG   Bust of Numerian l., laur., wearing cuirass ornamented with head of Medusa, and holding with r. hand sceptre and on l. arm shield, on which is a relief representing the Emperor on horseback, galloping r., over fallen barbarians: border of dots.

   Rev. MONETA A VGG   The three Monetæ l., each holding scales and cornucopiæ and having at her feet a conical heap of metal: border of dots.   Æ 1·4.   Pl. LIV. fig. 5.

   This medallion has been plated.

3. Obv. Same inscription.   Bust of Numerian r., laur., wearing cuirass and paludamentum edged on l. shoulder with fringe: border of dots.

   Rev. Same inscription and border, and similar type.   Æ 1·5.

   This medallion has been plated.

CARINUS.

(MARCVS AVRELIVS CARINVS.)

CAES. A.D. 282 : AUG. A.D. 283 : DIED A.D. 285.

1. Obv. M AVR CARINVS NOB CAES   Bust of Carinus r., bearded and laur., wearing cuirass and paludamentum edged on l. shoulder with fringe : border of dots.

    Rev. MO NETA AV GG   The three Monetæ l., each holding scales and cornucopiæ, and having at her feet a conical heap of metal : border of dots.   Æ 1·25.   Pl. LIV. fig. 2.

    This medallion has been plated.

2. Obv. Same inscription and border, and similar type.
    Rev. Same inscription and border, and similar type.
    Æ 1·2.   Pl. LIV. fig. 3.

    This medallion has been plated.

DIOCLETIAN.

(CAIVS VALERIVS DIOCLETIANVS.)

Aug. a.d. 284: Abd. a.d. 305: Died a.d. 313.

1. Obv. **IMP C C VAL DIOCLETIANVS P F AVG**   Head of Diocletian r., bare, bearded; below, a palm-branch incuse: border of dots.

   Rev. **IOVI CONS ERVATORI** (In exergue) **SMN** (Nicomedia)   Jupiter l., wearing pallium, which, hanging on his r. arm and l. shoulder, falls behind him; he holds on r. hand globe surmounted by Victory r., with wreath and palm, and leans with l. on sceptre; before him, at his feet, an eagle l., head r. with wreath in beak: border of dots.

   N 1·5.   Wt. 830·5 grs.   Pl. LV. fig. 1.

2. Obv. Same inscription and border, and similar type.

   Rev. **IOVI CONS ERVATORI** (In exergue) **ALE** (Alexandria)   Jupiter seated towards l. on throne, wearing pallium, and holding thunderbolt with r. hand and sceptre with l.; before him, at his feet, an eagle l., head r., with wreath in beak: border of dots.   Æ 1·35.

3. Obv. Same inscription. Bust of Diocletian r., bearded and laur., wearing cuirass and paludamentum edged on l. shoulder with fringe: border of dots.

   Rev. **MONETA AVG**   The three Monetæ, each holding scales and cornucopiæ, and having at her feet a conical heap of metal; the outer Monetæ stand l., the centre one faces: border of dots.

   Æ 1·55.   Pl. LV. fig. 2.

   This medallion is plated.

4. Obv. Same inscription and border, and similar type.

   Rev. **MONETA AVGG**   Same type and border.   Æ 1·4.

   This medallion is plated.

5. Obv. Same inscription. Bust of Diocletian l., laur., wearing tunica palmata and toga picta, and holding with r. hand sceptre surmounted by eagle: border of dots.

   Rev. Same inscription and similar type; the three Monetæ stand l.: border of dots.   Æ 1·35.

6. Obv. Same inscription. Bust of Diocletian r., bearded and laur., wearing cuirass ornamented with head of Medusa; from l. shoulder hangs the ægis: border of dots.

   Rev. **MONETA AV GG** Similar type, and same border. Æ 1·3.

   This medallion is plated and gilt.

7. Obv. Same inscription and similar type; Diocletian holding with l. hand parazonium: border of dots.

   Rev. **MONETA AVGG** Similar type, and same border.

   Æ 1·55. Pl. LV. 3.

8. Obv. **IMP C DIOCLETIANVS P F AVG** Bust of Diocletian r., bearded and laur., wearing paludamentum and cuirass: border of dots.

   Rev. **MO NETA AV GG** Similar type, and same border. Æ 1·2.

   This medallion is plated.

9. Obv. **IMP C C VAL DIOCLETIANVS P F AVG** Bust of Diocletian r., bearded and laur., wearing cuirass ornamented with head of Medusa; from l. shoulder hangs the ægis: border of dots.

   Rev. **MONETA IOVI ET HERCVLI AVG G** Juno Moneta, holding scales and cornucopiæ, standing l. between Jupiter before her, and Hercules behind her; at her feet, a conical heap of metal: Jupiter, facing, head r., with pallium over l. shoulder, holds sceptre and thunderbolt: Hercules, facing, head l., rests his r. hand on club, and holds apple in his l.; over his l. arm hangs the lion's skin: border of dots. Æ 1·35. Pl. LV. fig. 4.

MAXIMIAN I.

(MARCVS AVRELIVS VALERIVS MAXIMIANVS HERCVLIVS.)

Caes. a.d. **285** : Aug. a.d. 286 : Died a.d. 310.

1. Obv. IMP C M AVR V AL MAXIMIANVS P F AVG   Head of Maximian l., bearded, wearing lion's skin : border of dots.
   Rev. MONETA AVGG   The three Monetæ l., each holding scales and cornucopiæ, and **having at her feet a conical** heap of metal : border of dots.   Æ 1·65.   Pl. LVI. fig. 1.

2. Obv. IMP C M AVR VAL MAXIMIANVS P F AVG   Bust of Maximian l., bearded and laur., wearing tunica palmata and toga picta, holding with r. hand sceptre surmounted by eagle : border of dots.
   Rev. Same inscription and border, and similar type.   Æ 1·35.

3. Obv. IMP C M AVR VAL MAXIMIANVS AVG   Bust of Maximian r., bearded and laur., wearing cuirass and paludamentum edged on l. shoulder with fringe : border of dots.
   Rev. Same.   Æ 1·3.
   This medallion is plated.

4. Obv. VIRTVS MAXIMIANI AVG   Bust of Maximian l., bearded and laur., wearing cuirass ornamented with head of Medusa ; with r. hand he holds his horse by the bridle, and **on l.** arm carries shield, on which are represented the Wolf and Twins beneath the fig-tree : border of dots.
   Rev. Same inscription and border, and similar type.   Æ 1·6.   Pl. LVI. fig. **2**.
   This medallion is plated.

CONSTANTIUS I. (CHLORUS.)

(FLAVIVS VALERIVS CONSTANTIVS.)

Caes. a.d. 292: Aug. a.d. 305: Died a.d. 306.

1. Obv. IMP C FL VAL CONSTANTIVS P F AVG   Bust of Constantius r., bearded and laur., wearing cuirass and paludamentum edged on l. shoulder with fringe : border of dots.

    Rev. MON ETA A VGG   The three Monetæ, each holding scales and cornucopiæ, and having at her feet a conical heap of metal; the outer Monetæ stand l., the centre one faces: border of dots.   Æ 1·5.

2. Obv. VIRTVS CONSTANTI AV GT   Bust of Constantius l., bearded and laur., wearing cuirass; he holds spear ? with r. hand, and on l. arm, shield; over r. shoulder is the strap of the parazonium, the handle of which is visible; the shield is ornamented with a relief representing the Emperor on horseback l., preceded by Victory, and followed by a soldier armed with spear and shield : border of dots.

    Rev. MO NETA AV GG   Same type and border.

    Æ 1·5.   Pl. LVI. fig. 3.

    This medallion has been plated.

HELENA.

(FLAVIA IVLIA HELENA.)

DIED A.D. 328.

Obv. **FLAVIA AELENA AVGVSTA** (*Sic.*) Bust of Helena r., draped; her hair is wavy, and her head is encircled with a broad band, ornamented with a **wreath : border of dots.**

Rev. **PIETAS A V GVSTAE** Pietas l., wearing tunic and peplum; on l. arm she **holds** child, and with r. hand presents apple to another **before** her who raises his **hands :** border of dots.

Æ 1·55. Pl. LVI. fig. 4.

GALERIUS.

(GALERIVS VALERIVS MAXIMIANVS.)

CAES. A.D. 292: AUG. A.D. 305: DIED A.D. 311.

1. Obv. [MA]XIMIANV S NOB CAES   Bust of Galerius l., bearded and laur., holding spear with r. hand, and wearing ægis on l. shoulder.

    Rev. MONETA AV GG   The three Monetæ l., each holding scales and cornucopiæ, and having at her feet a conical heap of metal.   Æ 1·2.

2. Obv. GAL VAL MAXIMIANVS NOB C   Bust of Galerius r., bearded and laur., wearing paludamentum and cuirass: border of dots.

    Rev. MON ETA A VGG   Same type: border of dots.   Æ 1·3.

    This medallion has been plated.

3. Obv. GAL VAL MAXIMIANVS NOB CAES   Similar type and same border.

    Rev. MONETA AVGG   Similar type, and same border.

    Æ 1·4.   Pl. LVII. fig. 1.

    This medallion has been plated.

CONSTANTINE I.

(FLAVIVS GALERIVS VALERIVS CONSTANTINVS.)

CAES. A.D. 306: AUG. A.D. 308: DIED A.D. 337.

1. Obv. **D N CONSTANTINVS MAX AVG** Bust of Constantine r., laur., wearing tunica palmata and toga picta, and holding with r. hand sceptre surmounted by eagle, and on l. globe: border of dots.

    Rev. **S E N A T V S** (In exergue) **S M T S** (Thessalonica) Emperor l., laur., wearing toga edged with ornamented band; on r. hand he holds globe, and with l., by its head, sceptre; round his waist is an embroidered belt: border of dots.
    A' 1·3. Wt. 204 grs. Pl. LVII. fig. 2.

2. Obv. **CONSTANTI NVS MAX AVG** Bust of Constantine r., wearing laureate diadem, paludamentum, and cuirass: border of dots.

    Rev. **GLORIA SAE CVLI VIR TVS CAESS** (In exergue) **P R** (Rome) Constantine, as Jupiter, laur., and wearing pallium, seated l. on cuirass, holding sceptre with l. hand, and with r. receiving globe surmounted by phœnix r. from one of the Cæsars, who runs towards him, bearing trophy on l. shoulder, clad in paludamentum and cuirass; before him, a panther r., fawning on the Emperor: border of dots.
    Æ 1·55. Pl. LVII. fig. 3.

3. Obv. Same inscription and type.

    Rev. **VIRTVS AVG N** Emperor, wearing paludamentum and cuirass, on horse galloping r.; he is piercing with his spear a falling barbarian, looking back.
    Æ 1·4.

4. Obv. **CONSTANTI NOPOLIS** Bust of Constantinopolis l., wearing crested helmet ornamented with laurel-wreath, cuirass, and mantle; against her l. shoulder rests a sceptre: border of dots.

    Rev. **VICTORIA AV G GNN** Constantinopolis, turreted, and wearing tunic and peplum, seated l. on stool; she holds branch and cornucopiæ; behind her, Victory, facing, head l., wearing tunic and peplum, and holding wreath and palm border of dots.
    Æ 1·5. Pl. LVIII. fig. 1.

5. Obv. Same.
   Rev. **VICTORIA AVGVSTI** Constantinopolis, turreted, and wearing tunic and peplum, seated l. on stool; she holds branch and cornucopiæ: border of dots. Æ 1·45. Pl. LVIII. fig. 2.

6. Obv. **VRBS ROMA** Bust of Roma l., wearing crested helmet, cuirass, and mantle: border of dots.
   Rev. Wolf l. and Twins; above, two stars: border of dots.
   Æ 1·3. Pl. LVIII. fig. 3.

7. Obv. Same inscription and border, and similar type.
   Rev. Wolf r. and Twins within cave, on which are seated two shepherds, each holding pedum; above, two stars: border of dots.
   Æ 1·3. Pl. LVIII. fig. 4.

CONSTANTINE II.

(FLAVIVS CLAVDIVS IVLIVS CONSTANTINVS.)

Caes. a.d. 317: Aug. a.d. 337: Died a.d. 340.

1. Obv. FL CL CONSTANTINVS IVN NOB **CAES**   Bust of Constantine Junior r., laur., wearing paludamentum and cuirass: border of dots.

   Rev. PRINCIPIA IV **VENTVTIS** (In exergue) **SARMATIA** (Treves)
   T R
   Cæsar l., clad in paludamentum and cuirass, holding globe on r. hand, and leaning with l. on reversed spear; he places his r. foot on the l. knee of a Sarmatian captive in an attitude of supplication: border of dots. N 1·25.   Wt. 204·2 grs.   Pl. LIX. fig. 1.

2. Obv. **AVGVSTVS**   Head of Constantine I. or II? r., wearing laureate diadem: border of dots.

   Rev. **CAESAR**   Within laurel-wreath; beneath, **SIS** (Siscia): border of dots. R 1·5.   Wt. 197·3 grs.   Pl. LIX. fig. 2.

3. Obv. CONSTANTINVS IVN NOB C   Bust of Constantine Junior r., laur., wearing paludamentum and cuirass.

   Rev. **CONSTANTI NOPOLIS**   Constantinopolis, turreted, winged, and wearing peplum, seated l.; she holds branch and cornucopiæ: border of dots.   Æ 1·2.

CONSTANS.

(FLAVIVS IVLIVS CONSTANS.)

CAES. A.D. 333: AUG. A.D. 337: DIED A.D. 350.

1. Obv. **FL IVL CONSTANS PIVS FELIX AVG** Bust of Constans r., wearing laureate diadem, paludamentum, and cuirass: border of dots.
   Rev. **SALVS ET SPES REIPVB LICAE** (In exergue) **TES** (Thessalonica) The three Emperors, one, Constantine II? facing, between the other two, Constans and Constantius II? who are looking towards him; each wears paludamentum and cuirass, holds sceptre in r. hand, and rests l. on shield: border of dots.
   N' 1·55. Wt. 297 grs. Pl. LIX. fig. 3.

2. Obv. Same inscription and border, and similar type.
   Rev. **GAVDIVM POPVLI ROMANI** Laurel-wreath, within which, SIC V SIC X and beneath which, **TES** (Thessalonica): border of dots.
   Æ 1·5. Wt. 190·3 grs.

   This medallion is broken at the edge in two places.

3. Obv. Same inscription and border, and similar type.
   Rev. **TRIVMFATOR GENTIVM BARBARARVM** (In exergue) **TES** (Thessalonica) Constans l., clad in paludamentum and cuirass, holding vexillum with r. hand, and resting l. on shield: border of dots.
   Æ 1·7. Wt. 197·7 grs. Pl. LX. fig. 1.

4. Obv. **FL IVL CONS TANS P F AVG** Similar type, and same border.
   Rev. **TRIVMFATOR GEN[T] IVM BARBARARVM** (In exergue) **·SIS[·]** (Siscia) Constans l., clad in paludamentum and cuirass, holding labarum with r. hand and reversed spear with l.: border of dots.
   Æ 1·45. Wt. 159·1 grs.

   This medallion has lost much of its edge.

5. Obv. **FL IVL CONSTANS P F AVG** Similar type, and same border.
   Rev. **ROMA BEATA** Roma, helmeted, and clad in tunic and peplum, seated l. on shield; on r. hand she holds globe surmounted by Victory r., with wreath and palm, and with l. hand, spear: border of dots.
   Æ 1·3.

CONSTANS.

6. Obv. D N FL CONSTANS AVG Similar type, and same border.
   Rev. VICTO RIA AVG Victory, wearing tunic and peplum, seated r. on cuirass and shield, and inscribing with a stilus $\genfrac{}{}{0pt}{}{VOT}{XX}$ on another shield, which she holds with her l. hand, and which rests on her l. knee. Æ 1·2.

7. Obv. CONSTANS P F AVG Similar type, and same border.
   Rev. VICTORIA AVGG NN Similar type, Victory seated on cuirass only: border of dots. Æ 1·4. Pl. LX. fig. 2.

8. Obv. CONSTAN S P F AVG Bust of Constans r., wearing diadem with double row of pearls, paludamentum, and cuirass: border of dots.
   Rev. VIRTVS AVG Emperor r., clad in paludamentum and cuirass, holding spear and globe; before him, a captive, seated r., on the ground, looking back, his hands tied behind him: border of dots. Æ 1·35. Pl. LX. fig. 3.

CONSTANTIUS II.

(FLAVIVS IVLIVS CONSTANTIVS.)

CAES. A.D. 323: AUG. A.D. 337: DIED A.D. 361.

1. Obv. **FL IVL CONSTANTIVS NOB C**   Bust of Constantius I., laur., wearing paludamentum and cuirass: border of dots.

   Rev. **PRINCIPI IVVE NTVTIS** (In exergue) **CONS** (Constantinople) Cæsar l., clad in paludamentum and cuirass, holding vexillum and reversed spear; behind him, two signa: border of dots.

   N 1·5.   Wt. 310·5 grs.   Pl. LXI. fig. 1.

2. Obv. **D N CONSTAN TIVS MAX AVG**   Bust of Constantius II., three-quarter face l., wearing crested helmet bound with diadem of double row of pearls, paludamentum, and cuirass ornamented with head of Medusa; on r. hand he holds Victory r. bearing wreath, and with l. spear: border of dots.

   Rev. **GLORIA RO MANORVM** (In exergue) **S M N** (Nicomedia)   Female figure (City) seated l. on throne, her l. foot resting on prow; she wears tunic, peplum, and necklace, and her head is bound with fillet; on r. hand she holds globe surmounted by Victory r. bearing wreath and palm, and in l. hand, sceptre like thyrsus: border of dots.

   N 1·55.   Wt. 312·4 grs.   Pl. LXI. fig. 2.

3. Obv. **FL IVL CONSTAN TIVS PERP AVG**   Bust of Constantius II. l., wearing diadem with double row of pearls, paludamentum, and cuirass: border of dots.

   Rev. **GLORIA RO MANORVM** (In exergue) **S M ANT** (Antioch)   Similar type, and same border. N 1·45.   Wt. 302·2 grs.

4. Obv. **FL IVL CONSTANTI VS PIVS FELIX AVG**   Bust of Constantius II. r., wearing laureate diadem, paludamentum, and cuirass: border of dots.

   Rev. **GAVDIVM POP[VLI R]OMANI**   Laurel-wreath, within which, **SIC** / **X** / **SIC** / **XX**   and beneath which, **TES** (Thessalonica): border of dots.

   R 1·5.   Wt. 181·8 grs.

   This medallion has lost much of its edge.

CONSTANTIUS II. 91

5. Obv. **FL IVL CONSTAN TIVS P F AVG** Similar type, and same border.

   Rev. **GAVDIVM POPVLI ROMANI** Laurel-wreath, within which, **SIC** and beneath which, · **SIS** · (Siscia): border of dots.
   XX
   SIC
   XXX
   Æ 1·5. Wt. 209·6 grs. Pl. LXI. fig. 3.

6. Obv. Same inscription and border as no. 4, and similar type.

   Rev. **TRIVMFATOR GENTIVM BARBARARVM** (In exergue) **TES** (Thessalonica) Emperor l., clad in paludamentum and cuirass, holding vexillum with r. hand, and resting l. on shield: border of dots. Æ 1·5. Wt. 200·5 grs.

7. Obv. **FL IVL CONSTANTIVS NOB C** Bust of Constantius r., laur., wearing paludamentum and cuirass: border of dots.

   Rev. **VIRTVS CAESARVM** Cæsar, wearing paludamentum and cuirass, facing, head l.; he rests r. hand on trophy, and holds reversed spear with l.; at the foot of the trophy is a female figure, seated l., resting her head on her hands: border of dots. Æ 1·25. Pl. LXII. fig. 1.

8. Obv. **D N CONSTAN TIVS P F AVG** Bust of Constantius II. r., wearing diadem with double row of pearls, paludamentum, and cuirass: border of dots.

   Rev. **DEBELLATOR I GENTT** (In exergue) **BARBARA** Emperor, wearing **paludamentum and** cuirass, on horse prancing r.; he hurls his spear at a barbarian, armed with sword and shield, who kneels on l. knee in an attitude of defence: border of dots.
   Æ 1·35. Pl. LXII. fig. 2.

9. Obv. Same inscription. Bust of **Constantius II. r., wearing** laureate diadem, paludamentum, and cuirass.

   Rev. **LARGI TI[O]** Emperor, wearing **mantle, tunic, and** ornamented **girdle,** seated, facing, his feet on footstool; **in l. hand** he holds scroll, and with r. gives money to Constantinopolis, who, clad in tunic and peplum, and wearing radiate crown, bends forward to r. and raises her peplum to receive the gifts; on the other side of the Emperor stands Roma, facing, **head** l., helmeted, and wearing short doubled tunic which leaves r. breast bare; she holds spear with l. hand, and rests r. on the shoulders of the Emperor. Æ 1·45. Pl. LXII. fig. 3.

10. Obv. Same inscription. Bust **of Constantius II. r.,** wearing **diadem** with double row of pearls, paludamentum, **and cuirass.**

    Rev. **MONETA AVG** (In exergue) **R** (Roma) The three Monetæ l., each holding scales and cornucopiæ, and having at her feet a conical heap of metal. Æ 1·15.

11. Obv. **CONSTANTIVS P F AVG** Bust of Constantius II. r., wearing laureate diadem, paludamentum, and cuirass: border of dots.

Rev. **VICTORI A AVG NN** Victory, wearing peplum, seated r. on cuirass and shield, and inscribing with a stilus $\frac{VOT}{X}$ on another shield, which she holds with l. hand: border of dots. Æ 1·25. Pl. LXII. fig. 4.

12. Obv. **D N CONSTAN TIVS P F AVG** Bust of Constantius II. l., wearing laureate diadem, tunic, and toga, and raising r. hand: border of dots.

Rev. **VICTORIA AVG VSTORVM** Emperor, facing, head l., clad in paludamentum and cuirass, holding with l. hand spear; he is conducted by Victory l., looking back, who wears doubled tunic, and carries palm in r. hand: border of dots.

Æ 1·35. Pl. LXII. fig. 5.

13. Obv. Same inscription. Bust of Constantius II. r., wearing diadem with double row of pearls, paludamentum, and cuirass: border of dots.

Rev. **VICTORIA AVGVSTIN** Victory, wearing doubled tunic, advancing l., carrying wreath in extended r. hand, and dragging with l. an eastern captive after her: border of dots. Æ 1·25.

14. Obv. Same inscription and border, and similar type.

Rev. **VIRTV S AVG N** Emperor, laur., clad in paludamentum and cuirass, holding spear and globe, standing r. between two naked captives, seated on the ground, both looking back; the one on l. has his hands tied behind him: border of dots. Æ 1·2.

MAGNENTIUS.

(FLAVIVS MAGNVS MAGNENTIVS.)

Aug. a.d. 350: Died a.d. 353.

1. Obv. **IM CAE MAGN ENTIVS AVG** Bust of Magnentius r., bare-headed, wearing paludamentum and cuirass: border of dots.

   Rev. **SECVRITAS REIPVBLICAE** (In exergue) **TR** (Treves) Securitas, facing, head r., with l. leg crossed in front of r., leaning with l. arm on a column, and raising r. hand above her head; she wears stephane, tunic, and peplum, armlets, and bracelets: border of dots.
   Æ 1·5. Wt. 198·7 grs. Pl. LXIII. fig. 1.

2. Obv. Same. (Same die.)

   Rev. Same inscription and border, and similar type. Æ 1·5. Wt. 199·8 grs.

3. Obv. **IMP CAE MAGN ENTIVS AVG** Similar type, and same border.

   Rev. **VICTO RIA·AVGG·** Emperor l., wearing paludamentum and cuirass; he holds on his r. hand globe, surmounted by Victory r. with wreath and palm, and in his l., spear; he is crowned by Victory, behind him, wearing doubled tunic, and holding palm in l. hand: border of dots.
   Æ 1·25. Pl. LXIII. fig. 2.

4. Obv. Same. (Same die.)

   Rev. **VICTOR IA·AVGG·** Victory l., wearing doubled tunic, and holding wreath and palm; with her r. foot she strikes a bearded captive, his hands tied behind him, who kneels l. on r. knee and looks back: border of dots.
   Æ 1·35. Pl. LXIII. fig. 3

DECENTIUS.

(MAGNVS DECENTIVS.)

Caes. a.d. 351: Died a.d. 353.

1. Obv. MAG DECENTI VS NOB CAES   Bust of Decentius r., bare-headed, wearing paludamentum and cuirass: border of dots.

    Rev. VICTOR IA·AVGG· Victory l., wearing doubled tunic, and holding wreath and palm; with her r. foot she strikes a bearded captive, his hands tied behind him, who kneels l. on r. knee and looks back: border of dots.   Æ 1·3.   Pl. LXIII. fig. 4.

    (The rev. from the same die as Magnentius, no. 4.)

2. Obv. Same inscription. Bust of Decentius r., bare-headed, wearing paludamentum and cuirass, and holding spear with r. hand, and on l., globe surmounted by Victory l. with wreath and palm.

    Rev. [VIRT] VS AVGG Emperor, wearing paludamentum and cuirass, on horse galloping r.; he is about to strike with his spear a barbarian, who, falling on l. knee, raises his l. hand and holds spear with r.

       Æ 1·3.   Pl. LXIV. fig. 1.

3. Obv. IMP CAES DEC ENTIVS AVG   Bust of Decentius r., bare-headed, wearing paludamentum and cuirass: border of dots.

    Rev. Same as no. 1. (Same die.)   .   Æ 1·35.

CONSTANTIUS GALLUS.

(FLAVIVS CLAVDIVS IVLIVS CONSTANTIVS.)

Caes. a.d. 351: Died a.d. 354.

1. Obv. **D N FL CL CONSTANTIVS NOB CAES** Bust of Constantius Gallus r., bare-headed, wearing paludamentum and cuirass: border of dots.
   Rev. **GLORIA ROMANORVM** Victory, wearing doubled tunic, advancing l., carrying wreath and palm: border of dots. Æ 1·3.

2. Obv. Same. (Same die.)
   Rev. **VRBS ROMA** Roma, helmeted, and wearing tunic and peplum, seated l. on shield; on r. hand she holds globe surmounted by Victory r. bearing wreath and palm, and with l. hand, spear: border of dots. Æ 1·2. **Pl. LXIV. fig. 2.**

JULIAN II.

(FLAVIVS CLAVDIVS IVLIANVS.)

Caes. a.d. 355 : Aug. a.d. 360 : Died a.d. 363.

Obv. D N CL IVL IANVS N C   Bust of Julian r., bare-headed, wearing cuirass ornamented with head of Medusa, and paludamentum fastened on l. shoulder with a large fibula : border of dots.

Rev. VIRTV S AVG N   Caesar, clad in paludamentum and cuirass, holding branch and vexillum, standing l. and placing his r. foot on the back of an eastern captive, seated l. on the ground, looking back : border of dots.   Æ 1·2.   Pl. LXIV. fig. 3.

VALENTINIAN I.

(VALENTINIANVS.)

Aug. A.D. 364: Died A.D. 375.

1. Obv. D N VALENTINI ANVS P F AVG Bust of Valentinian r., wearing diadem with double row of pearls, paludamentum, and cuirass: border of dots.

   Rev. GLORIA RO MANORVM (In exergue) SMTR (Treves) Roma and Constantinopolis seated on thrones; Roma, facing, wears helmet, doubled tunic which leaves r. breast bare, and peplum; she holds on r. hand globe surmounted by Victory r., and in l. hand, sceptre; Constantinopolis l., turreted, wears tunic and peplum, rests r. foot on prow, and holds on r. hand globe surmounted by Victory r., and with l. hand, cornucopiæ border of dots.

   N 1·2.   Wt. 201·5 grs.   Pl. LXIV. fig. 4.

   This medallion is set in a beaded rim.

2. Obv. Same inscription and border, and similar type.

   Rev. VICTORIA AVGVSTORVM (In exergue) ROMA (Rome) Victory, clad in doubled tunic, advancing r. and looking back; on l. shoulder she carries trophy, and with r. hand drags after her, by the hair, a captivo, whose hands are tied behind him: border of dots.   Æ 1·15.

VALENS.

Aug. a.d. 364: Died a.d. 378.

1. Obv. **DNVALEN SPFAVG** Bust of Valens r., wearing diadem with double row of pearls, paludamentum, and cuirass: border of dots.

   Rev. **TRIVMFATOR GENT BARB** (In exergue) **TRPS·** (Treves) Emperor, facing, head l., wearing diadem with double row of pearls, paludamentum, and cuirass, and holding labarum and globe; on his r., a captive, kneeling l. on l. knee and looking back, his hands tied behind him: border of dots.

                                    AR 1·5. Wt. 207·9 grs. Pl. LXV. fig. 1.

2. Obv. Same inscription and border, and similar type.

   Rev. **RES[TI]TVTOR REIP[VB]LICAE** (In exergue) **R P** (Roma) Emperor, facing, head r., wearing paludamentum and cuirass, and holding vexillum and globe surmounted by Victory l. with wreath and palm: border of dots.   Æ 1·15.

GRATIAN.

(GRATIANVS.)

Aug. a.d. 367 : Died a.d. 383.

1. Obv. D N GRATIA NVS P F AVG Bust of Gratian r., wearing diadem with double row of pearls, paludamentum, and cuirass: border of dots.

    Rev. GLORIA RO MANORVM (In exergue) TROBT (Treves) Roma, facing, seated on throne, wearing helmet, tunic, and peplum, and holding globe and reversed spear: border of dots.

    N 1·55.   Wt. 308·2 grs.   Pl. LXV. fig. 2.

    This medallion has been worn as an ornament, and part of a loop, which has been added to it, remains.

2. Obv. Same inscription and border, and similar type.

    Rev. VRBS ROMA (In exergue) R P ? (Rome) Roma, seated l. on throne, wearing helmet, tunic, and peplum, and holding globe and spear; at her side, a shield.   Æ 1·1.

HONORIUS.

Aug. a.d. 393: Died a.d. 423.

1. Obv. DN HONORI VS P F AVG Bust of Honorius r., wearing diadem with double row of pearls, paludamentum, and cuirass: border of dots.

    Rev. GLORIA RO MANORVM (In exergue) COMOB (In field) R M (Rome) Roma, facing, seated on throne, wearing helmet, necklace, armlets, and bracelets, and robed in tunic which leaves r. breast bare, and peplum; she holds globe and reversed spear: border of dots. N 1·45. Wt. 328·5 grs. Pl. LXV. fig. 3.

    This medallion has a ring attached to it, having been worn as an ornament.

2. Obv. Same.

    Rev. TRIVMFATOR GENT BARB (In exergue) RM PS (Rome) Emperor, facing, head l., wearing diadem, paludamentum, and cuirass, and holding labarum and globe; on his r., a captive, crouching l. and looking back, his hands tied behind him: border of dots.
    R 1·6. Wt. 193·8 grs.

ATTALUS.

(PRISCVS ATTALVS.)

Aug. a.d. 414 : Dethroned a.d. 416.

Obv. **PRISCVSATTA LVSPFAVG** Bust of Attalus r., wearing diadem with row of jewels between double row of pearls, paludamentum, and cuirass : border of dots.

Rev. **INVICTARO MAAETERNA (In** exergue) **RMPS** (Rome) Roma, facing, seated **on** throne ornamented with two lions' heads; she **is** helmeted, and wears necklace, armlet, and bracelets, and is robed in tunic which leaves **r.** breast bare, and peplum, one end of which hangs over **her** l. arm and is fastened with a fibula; on r. hand she holds globe surmounted **by Victory r.** bearing wreath and palm, and with l., reversed **spear:** border **of dots.**

$\mathcal{R}$ 2. Wt. 1202·5 grs. Pl. LXVI.

INDEX I.

NAMES.

Aelius Caesar, p. 6.
Antoninus Pius, p. 7.
Attalus, p. 101.
Aurelius, **Marcus**, p. 13.
Aurelius, **Marcus**, and **Commodus**, p. 15.

Caracalla, p. 35.
Carinus, p. 78.
Carus, p. 76.
Claudius II. (Gothicus), p. 71.
Commodus, p. 21.
Commodus and Annius Verus, p. 20.
Commodus and Crispina, p. 31.
Commodus and Marcus Aurelius, p. 15.
Constans, p. 88.
Constantine I. p. 85.
Constantine II. p. 87.
Constantius I. (Chlorus), p. 82.
Constantius II. p. 90.
Constantius **Gallus**, p. 95.
Crispina and **Commodus**, p. 31.

Decentius, p. 94.
Diocletian, p. 79.
Domitian, p. 1.
Domna, Julia, p. 34.

Elagabalus, p. 37.

Faustina the Elder, p. 12.
Faustina the Younger, p. 16.
Florianus, p. 73.

Galerius, p. 84.
Gallienus, p. 64.
Gallienus and Salonina, p. 67.
Gallienus and Saloninus, p. 68.
Gallienus and Valerian, p. 63.
Gallienus, Valerian, Valerian the Younger, and Salonina, p. 62.
Gallus, p. 57.
Gallus and Volusian, p. 59.
Geta, p. 36.
Gordian III. p. 45.
Gratian, p. 99.

Hadrian, p. 3.
Helena, p. 83.
Honorius, p. 100.

Julian II. p. 96.

Lucilla, p. 19.

Magnentius, p. 93.
Mamaea, Julia, p. 42.
Mamaea, Julia, and Severus Alexander, p. 41.
Maximian I. p. 81.
Maximin I. p. 43.

Numerian, p. 77.

Otacilia, p. 51.
Otacilia, Philip I., and Philip II. p. 53 ; 55.

Philip I. p. 50.
Philip I. and Philip II. p. 52.
Philip I., Otacilia, and Philip II. p. 53 ; 55.

Philip II. p. 56.
Philip II. and Philip I. p. 52.
Philip II., Philip I., and Otacilia, p. 53 ; 55.
Probus, p. 74.
Pupienus, p. 44.

Salonina, p. 69.
Salonina and Gallienus, p. 67.
Salonina, Valerian, Valerian the Younger, and Gallienus, p. 62.
Saloninus, p. 70.
Saloninus and Gallienus, **p. 68.**
Severus Alexander, p. 38.
Severus Alexander and **Julia Mamaea, p. 41.**
Severus, Septimius, p. **32.**

Tacitus, p. 72.
Trajan, p. **2.**

Valens, p. 98.
Valentinian I. p. 97.
Valerian, p. 61.
Valerian and Gallienus, **p. 63.**
Valerian, Valerian the **Younger, Gallienus,** and Salonina, p. 62.
Valerian the Younger, Valerian, Gallienus, and **Salonina,** p. 62.
Verus, Annius, and **Commodus, p. 20.**
Verus, Lucius, p. 18.
Volusian, p. 60.
Volusian and Gallus, p. 59.

INDEX II.

REVERSE-INSCRIPTIONS.

A.

ADLOCVTIO . AVG. Tacit.
ADLOCVTIO . AVGG. Numer. 1.
ADLOCVTIO . AVGVSTI. Gord. III. 6; 7; 8; 9.
ADVENTVS . AVG . S . P . Q . R . OPT . PRINCIPI. Traj. 1.
ADVENTVS . AVGG. Phil. I. and Phil. II.; Volus. 2: Gallien. and Salonina, 3; Gallien. and Saloninus.
AEQVITAS . AVGVSTI. Elagab. 1: Sev. Alex. 1: Maximin I.: Gord. III. 1; 10.
AEQVITAS . PVBLICA. Gallien. and Salonina, 4: Salonina, 1; 2.
AESCVLAPIVS. Ant. Pius, 4; 5.
AETERNITAS. Faust. Sen. 2.
ANNONA . AVGVSTI . CERES . COS . III . P . P. Hadr. 3.
ARNAZI. Gallus. 4: Volus. 4.

B.

BRITANNIA . P . M . TR . P . X . IMP . VII . COS . IIII . P . P. Com. 12.

C.

CAESAR. Constantine II. 2.
CERES. Jul. Dom. 1.
CONCORDIA . AVGVSTORVM. Valer., Valer. Jun., Gallien. and Salonina.
CONCORDIA . COS . II. Hadr. 4 : Ael. Caes.
CONCORDIA . MILITVM. Geta.
CONSTANTINOPOLIS. Constantine II. 3.
CORNELIA . SALONINA . AVGVSTA. Gallien. and Salonina, 1 ; 2.
COS . III. Hadr. 5 ; 6 ; 7 ; 8 : L. Ver. 5.
COS . III . P . P. Hadr. 9 ; 10 ; 11 ; 12.
COS . IIII. Ant. Pius, 9 ; 16 ; 17 ; 18 ; 22 ; 24.
COS . VI. Com. 29.

D.

DEBELLATORI . GENTT . BARBARA. Constantius II. 8.
DIS . AVSPICIBVS . P . M . TR . P . III . COS . I . P. P. Sept. Sev. 2.
DIVI . M . PII . F . P . M . TR . P . IIII . COS . II P . P. Sept. Sev. 5.

E.

EX . ORACVLO . APOLLINIS. Phil. I., Otacil., and Phil. II. 3.

F.

FECVNDITATI . AVG. Jul. Dom. 2.
FELICITAS . PERPETVA. Jul. Mam. 1 ; 2.
FELICITAS . TEMPORVM. Sev. Alex. and Jul. Mam. 1 ; 2.
FIDES . EXERCITVS. Gord. III. 11.
FIDES . MILITVM. Sev. Alex. 6 ; 7 : Sev. Alex. and Jul. Mam. 3 ; 4 : Gallien. 4.
FORTVNAE . REDVCI. Gallus and Volus. 1.
FORTVNAE . REDVCI . C . V . P . P. Com. 18.

G.

GAVDIVM . POPVLI . ROMANI . SIC . V . SIC . X. Constans, 2.
GAVDIVM . POPVLI . ROMANI . SIC . X . SIC . XX. Constantius II. 4.
GAVDIVM . POPVLI . ROMANI . SIC . XX . SIC . XXX. Constantius II. 5.
GLORIA . ROMANORVM. Constantius II. 2; 3: Const. Gal. 1: Valentinian I. 1: Grat. 1: Honor. 1.
GLORIA . SAECVLI . VIRTVS . CAESS. Constantino I. 2.

H.

HERC . ROM . CONDITORI . P. M . TR . P . XVIII . COS . VII . P. P. Com. 41; 42.
HERCVLI . ROMANO . AVG . P. M . TR . P . XVIII . COS . VII . P. P. Com. 37; 38; 39; 40.
HERCVLI . ROMANO . AVGV. Com. 43.

I.

IMP . II . COS . P. P. VOTA . PVBLICA. Com. 3.
IMP . II . COS . II . P. P. Com. 4.
IMP . III . COS . II . P. P. Com. 5.
IMP . VI . COS . III . GERMANIA . SVBACTA. M. Aur. 13.
IMP . VI . COS . III . VICT . GERM. M. Aur. 14.
IMP . VIII . COS . XI . CENS . POT . P. P. Domit. 1.
IMP . VIIII . COS . XI . CENS . POT . P. P. Domit. 2.
IMP . XXI . COS . XVI . CENS . P. P. P. Domit. 3.
INVICTA . ROMA . AETERNA. Attalus.
IOV . IVVENI . P. M . TR . P . XIIII . IMP . VIII . COS . V . P. P. Com. 24.
IOVI . CONSERVATORI. Diocl. 1; 2.
IVNONI . MARTIALI. Gallus, 1; 5: Gallus and Volus. 2.

L.

LARGITIO. Constantius II. 9.
LIBERALITAS . AVGG. Valer. and Gallien.
LIBERALITAS . AVGG . I. Valer. 3.
LIBERALITAS . AVGVSTI . II. Gord. III. 12.
LIBERALITAS . AVGVSTORVM. Pupien.

M.

MART . PACAT . P . M . TR . P . XIIII . IMP . VIII . COS . V . P . P. Com. 25.
MATER . CASTRORVM. Jul. Mam. 3.
MINER . VICT . P . M . TR . P . XIIII . IMP . VIII . COS . V . P . P. Com. 26; 27.
MONETA . AVG. Gallien. 1; 5; 6; 7: Claud. II. 2; 3: Florian: Prob. 1; 2; 3; 4; 5; 6; 7: Diocl. 3: Constantius II. 10.
MONETA . AVGG. Gallus, 2; 3: Volus. 1: Valer. 1: Gallien. 8; 9: Carus: Numer. 2; 3: Carinus, 1; 2: Diocl. 4; 5; 6; 7; 8: Maximian I. 1; 2; 3; 4: Constantius I. 1; 2: Galer. 1; 2; 3.
MONETA . IOVI . ET . HERCVLI . AVGG. Diocl. 9.
MONETAE . AVGG. Valer. 2.
MVNIFICENTIA . GORDIANI . AVG. Gord. III. 13.

O.

OB . CONSERVATIONEM . SALVTIS. Gallien. 10.
OB . LIBERTATEM . RECEPTAM. Gallien. 11.

P.

PAX . AETERNA. Gord. III. 14.
PAX . AVG. Gallien. 12.
PAX . AVG . S . C. Gallien. 2.
PIETAS . AVGVSTAE. Helena.
PIETAS . AVGVSTORVM . III . ET . II . COS. Otacil., Phil. I., and Phil. II. 1; 2.

PIO.IMP.OMNIA FELICIA.P.M.TR.P.XV.IMP.VIII.COS.VI.P.P.
    Com. 30.
P.M.TR.P.II.COS.P.P.   Claud. II. 1.
P.M.TR.P.III.COS.P.P.   Phil. I., Otacil., and Phil. II. 1.
P.M.TR.P.III.COS.II.P.P.FIDEI.MILIT.   Sept. Sev. 1; 3.
P.M.TR.P.VII.COS.II.P.P.   Gord. III. 5.
P.M.TR.P.VIIII.COS.III.P.P.VICT.AVG.   Sev. Alex. 4.
P.M.TR.P.VIIII.IMP.VI.COS.IIII.P.P.   Com. 9; 11.
P.M.TR.P.X.IMP.VII.COS.IIII.P.P.   Com. 13; 14; 15.
P.M.TR.P.X.IMP.VII.COS.IIII.VICT.BRIT.   Com. 16; 17.
P.M.TR.P.XI.COS.V.P.P.   Com. 19.
P.M.TR.P.XII.IMP.VIII.COS.V.P.P.TELLVS.STABIL.   Com. 20.
P.M.TR.P.XII.IMP.VIII.COS.V.PROVID.AVG.   Com. 22.
P.M.TR.P.XII.IMP.VIII.TELLVS.STABIL.COS.V.P.P.   Com. 21.
P.M.TR.P.XIII.IMP.VIII.COS.V.P.P.   Com. 23.
P.M.TR.P.XV.IMP.VIII.COS.VI.P.P.   Com. 31.
P.M.TR.P.XVI.IMP.VIII.COS.VI.P.P.   Com. 32.
P.M.TR.P.XVII.IMP.VIII.COS.VII.P.P.   Com. 33; 34; 35; 36.
P.M.TR.POT.COS.II.   Ant. Pius, 3.
PONT.MAX.TR.POT.COS.II.   Ant. Pius, 1.
PONT.MAX.TR.POT.COS.III.   Hadr. 1; 2.
PONTIF.MAX.TR.P.II.COS.P.P.   Sev. Alex. 2.
PONTIF.MAX.TR.P.V.COS.II.P.P.LIB.AVG.III.   Sev. Alex. 3.
PONTIF.MAX.TR.P.X.COS.III.P.P.PROF.AVG.   Sev. Alex. 5:
    Sev. Alex. and Jul. Mam. 5.
PONTIFEX.MAX.TR.P.IIII.COS.II.P.P.   Gord. III. 3; 4: Phil. I.,
    Otacil., and Phil. II. 2.
PRINCIPI.IVVENTVTIS.   Phil. II.: Saloninus, 1; 2: Constantius II. 1.
PRINCIPIA.IVVENTVTIS.SARMATIA.   Constantine II. 1.
PROFECTIO.AVG.COS.III.   M. Aur. 12.
PVDICITIA.AVG.   Otacil. 1; 2: Salonina, 3.

R.

RESTITVTOR.REIPVBLICAE.   Valens, 2.
ROMA.BEATA.   Constans, 5.
ROMAE.AETERNAE.   Sev. Alex. 8.

S.

SAECVLVM . NOVVM. Phil. I., Otacil., and Phil. II. 4.
SALVS . ET . SPES . REIPVBLICAE. Constans, 1.
SECVRIT . PVB . P . M . TR . P . XIIII . IMP . VIII . COS . V . P . P. Com. 28.
SECVRITAS. Faust. Sen. 3.
SECVRITAS . REIPVBLICAE. Magnen. 1; 2.
SENATVS. Constantine I. 1.
SEVERI . AVG . PII . FIL. Caracal.
SIDERIBVS . RECEPTA. Faust. Jun. 8.
SPES . PVBLICA. Sev. Alex. 9.

T.

TELLVS . STABIL. Hadr. 17.
TEMPORVM . FELICITAS. M. Aur. 3: Com. and Ann. Ver.: Jul. Mam. 4.
TRAIECTVS . AVG. Gord. III. 15.
TRIVMFATOR . GENT . BARB. Valens, 1: Honor. 2.
TRIVMFATOR . GENTIVM . BARBARARVM. Constans, 3; 4: Constantius II. 6.
TR . P . VI . IMP . III . COS . II. L. Ver. 1.
TR . P . VII . IMP . IIII . COS . III. L. Ver. 2.
TR . P . VII . IMP . IIII . COS . V . P . P. Traj. 3.
TR . P . VIII . IMP . IIII . COS . III. L. Ver. 3; 4.
TR . P . VIII . IMP . V . COS . IIII . P . P. Com. 6; 7.
TR . P . VIII . IMP . V . COS . IIII . P . P . VIRTVTI . AVG. Com. 8.
TR . P . VIIII . IMP . VI . COS . IIII . P . P. Com. 10.
TR . P . XX . IMP . III . COS . III. M. Aur. 9.
TR . P . XXII . IMP . IIII . COS . III. M. Aur. 10.
TR . P . XXIII . IMP . V . COS . III. M. Aur. 11.
TR . POT . COS. Com. 1; 2.
TR . POT . COS . II . P . P. Ant. Pius, 2.
TR . POT . III . COS . II. M. Aur. 4.
TR . POT . VIIII . COS . II. M. Aur. 5.
TR . POT . XIII . COS . II. M. Aur. 6.
TR . POT . XXI . COS . IIII. Ant. Pius, 21.

V.

VENERI . GENETRICI. Hadr. 13.
VICT . AVG . TR . P . III . COS . II . P . P. Sept. Sev. 4.
VICTORIA . AVG. ΝΕΙΚΗ . ΟΠΛΟΦΟΡΟC. Gord. III. 16.
VICTORIA . AVG . NN . VOT . X. Constantius II. 11.
VICTORIA . AVG . VOT . XX. Constans, 6.
VICTORIA . AVGG. Magnen. 3; 4: Decen. 1; 3.
VICTORIA . AVGG . NN. Constantine I. 4.
VICTORIA . AVGG . NN . VOT . XX. Constans, 7.
VICTORIA . AVGVSTI. Constantine I. 5.
VICTORIA . AVGVSTI . N. Constantius II. 13.
VICTORIA . AVGVSTORVM. Valer. 4: Constantius II. 12: Valentinian I. 2.
VIRTVS . AVG. Gallien. 3; 13: Constans, 8.
VIRTVS . AVG . N. Constantine I. 3: Constantius II. 14: Julian II.
VIRTVS . AVGG. Decen. 2.
VIRTVS . AVGVSTI. Gord. III. 2; 17: Phil. I.
VIRTVS . AVGVSTORVM. Volus. 3.
VIRTVS . CAESARVM. Constantius II. 7.
VIRTVTI . AVGVSTI. Hadr. 18.
VOT . SVSC . DEC . III . COS . IIII. Ant. Pius, 23.
VOTA . PVBLICA. Com. and Crisp.
VOTIS . DECENNALIBVS. Gallien. 14.
VOTIS . FELICIBVS. Com. 44; 45; 46.
VRBS . ROMA. Const. Gal. 2: Grat. 2.
VRBS . ROMA . AETERNA. Traj. 2.

INDEX III.

MINTS.

Alexandria, **ALE**. Diocl. 2.

Antioch, **S . M . ANT**. Constantius II. 3.

Constantinople, **CONS**. Constantius II. 1.

Nicomedia, **S . M . N**. Diocl. 1 : Constantius II. 2.

Roma, **P . R**. Constantine I. 2.
    R. Constantius II. 10.
    R . M. Honor. 1.
    R . M . P . S. Honor. 2 : Attalus.
    ROMA. Valentinian I. 2.
    R . P. Valens, 2.
    R . P? Grat. 2.

Siscia, **SIS**. Constantine II. 2 : Constans, 4 : Constantius II. 5.

Thessalonica, **S . M . TS**. Constantine I. 1.
    TES. Constans, 1 ; 2 ; 3 : Constantius II. 4 ; 6.

Treves, **S . M . TR**. Valentinian I. 1.
    TR. Constantine II. 1 : Magnen. 1 ; 2.
    TR . OB . T. Grat. 1.
    TR . P . S. Valens, 1.

INDEX IV.

TYPES.*

A.

Acerra, Traj. 2 : Lucil. 3 : Com. 7.

Adlocutio, Sept. Sev. 1 ; 3: Gord. III. 6 ; 7 ; 8 ; 9 : Tacit.: Numer. 1.

Adventus, Traj. 1 : Phil. I. and Phil. II. : Volus. 2 : Gallien. and Salonina, 2 : Gallien. and Saloninus.

Aedituus ? Traj. 2.

Aeneas with **Anchises and Iulus on shield of Venus** Genetrix, Hadr. 13.

Aesculapius, **Hadr. 15.**

,, aud Salus, Hadr. 6 ; 7.

,, arrival **of Serpent of, in the** Tiber, Ant. Pius, 4 ; 5.

Aeternitas, Faust. **Sen. 2.**

Africa with lion, **Com. 29.**

Alexandria, **return of fleet from, Com. 44 ; 45 ; 46.**

Amalthea carrying Jupiter, **Ant. Pius, 18.**

Anchises ; see Aeneas.

Annona and **Ceres, Hadr. 3.**

Anvil of Vulcan, Faust. Sen. 6.

Aplustre of trireme in form of elephant's head, Gord. III. 15.

Apollo standing on mountain, Gallus, 4 : Volus. 4.

,, Citharœdus, Hadr. 14 : Ant. Pius, 3.

,, ,, before tripod with Python, M. Aur. 4.

Armenia and Parthia, conquest of, L. Ver. 2.

Asiatic Campaign, Gord. III. 11.

" Aspergillum," Caracal.

Attica, contest for ; see Neptune and Minerva.

Aurelius ; see Marcus Aurelius.

---

* References to historical and legendary events are printed in spread type.

B.

Bacchus and Hercules, Sept. Sev. 2.
Barbarian slain by Emperor, Constantius II. 8 : Decen. 2.
Biga driven by Faustina, Faust. Sen. 4.
,, of Victory, Ant. Pius, 3.
Boar-hunt, Hadr. 10 : M. Aur. 2.
Bow, club, and quiver of Hercules, Com. 43.
Britain, conquest in, Com. 12 ; 16 ; 17.
Britannia Romana, Com. 12.
Bull sacrificed by Victory, Ant. Pius, 15.
Buoy? Com. 44 ; 45 ; 46.

C.

Caesar and captive, Constantine II. 7.
,, ,, Sarmatian captive, Constantine II. 1.
,, ,, standards, Geta.
,, crowned by Mars, Phil. II.
,, holding globe and spear, Saloninus, 1 ; 2.
,, ,, vexillum and spear, Constantius II. 1.
,, hunting boar, M. Aur. 2.
,, Mars, and Roma, Phil. II.
Camillus, Traj. 2 : Ant. Pius, 23 : Com. 3 ; 7.
Captive and Emperor, Valens, 1 : Honor. 2.
,, ,, Victory, Magnen. 4 : Decen. 1 ; 3.
,, at feet of Caesar, Saloninus, 1 ; 2.
,, ,, Emperor, Constans, 8.
,, dragged by Victory, Valentinian I. 2.
,, Eastern, and Emperor, Jul. II.
,, ,, dragged by Victory, Constantius II. 13.
,, king, of Parthia ? L. Ver. 2.
Captives and Emperor, Constantius II. 14.
,, seated beneath trophy, M. Aur. 13.
,, woman and youth, before trophy, Ant. Pius, 6.
Castor holding horse, M. Aur. 5.
Centaurs, representing Seasons, drawing quadriga of Hercules, M. Aur. 3.

Ceres and Annona, Hadr. 3.
," ," Lucilla, Lucil. 1.
," ," Neptune, Ant. Pius, 21.
," before altar, Jul. Dom. 1.
," presenting ears of corn to Emperor, Ant. Pius, 16.
Chariot, triumphal, Gord. III. 5.
Circus Maximus, **Gord. III. 5.**
Cista, Hadr. 3 : Lucil. 1.
Club, bow, and quiver of Hercules, Com. 43.
Colosseum or Flavian Amphitheatre, Sev. Alex. 2 : Gord. III. 13.
Column, rostral, Domit. 3.
," with figure of Apollo ? **Hadr. 6 ; 7.**
Commodus, Africa, and Victory, **Com. 29.**
Concordia, Hadr. 4 : Ael. Caes. : **Com. and Crisp. : Geta.**
," of Commodus and Crispina, **Com. and Crisp.**
," of Hadrian and Aelius Caesar, Hadr. 4 : Ael. Caes.
Congiarium, Sev. **Alex. 3 : Pupien. :** Gord. III. 12 : Valer. 3 : Valer. and Gallien.
Constans, Constantine **II., and Constantius II., Constans, 1.**
Constantine **I., as Jupiter, receiving phœnix,** Constantine I. 2.
Constantine **II., Constans, and Constantius II.,** Constans, 1.
Constantinopolis, **Constantine I. 4 ; 5 :** Constantine II. 3.
," and Roma, Valentinian **I. 1.**
," bust of, Constantine **I. 4 ; 5.**
," **Constantius II., and Roma,** Constantius II. 9.
," receiving money from Emperor, Constantius II. 9.
Constantius **II., Constantine II., and Constans, Constans, 1.**
," ," Constantinopolis, and **Roma, Constantius II. 9.**
Cow with Tellus, Ant. Pius, 14.
Cupids in garden, Faust. Jun. 2.
Cybele seated on lion, Faust. Sen. **1 ; 5 :** Lucil. 2.

D.

Diana as Hecate, (Faustina,) Faust. Jun. 8.
," before fountain, returned from chase, Faust. Jun. 1.
," Lucifera, riding on panther, Ant. Pius, 10.
," Venatrix, Ant. Pius, 9.

Diana? holding sceptre and fawn? Aut. Pius, 11.
Dog, the, bearing Isis Sothis, Faust. Jun. 3.
Dove of Venus, Faust. Jun. 6.

E.

Eagle of Jupiter, Sev. Alex. 6: Sev. Alex. and Jul. Mam. 3: Diocl. 1; 2.
,, on thunderbolt, Hadr. 8.
,, peacock, and owl, Hadr. 8.
Emperor and captive, Constans, 8: Valens, 1: Honor. 2.
    ,, ,, captives, Constantius II. 14.
    ,, ,, Eastern captive, Jul. II.
    ,, between standards, Hadr. 9.
    ,, conducted by Victory, Constantius II. 12.
    ,, crowned by Roma, Gord. III. 2.
    ,, ,, ,, soldier, Phil. I.: Volus. 3.
    ,, ,, ,, Victory, Ant. Pius, 16: Com. 31; 32: Sev. Alex. 4: Sev. Alex. and Jul. Mam. 1; 2: Gord. III. 3; 4; 5; 11; 14; 17: Phil. I., Otacil., and Phil. II. 2: Gallien. 13: Magnen. 3.
    ,, giving money to Constantinopolis, Constantius II. 9.
    ,, holding globe and sceptre, Constantine I. 1.
    ,, ,, labarum and spear, Constans, 4.
    ,, ,, trophy, and crowned by Victory, Gallien. 13.
    ,, ,, vexillum and globe, Valens, 2.
    ,, ,, vexillum and shield, Constans, 3: Constantius II. 6.
    ,, ,, Victory, Com. 13: and *passim*.
    ,, hunting boar, Hadr. 10.
    ,, ,, lion, Hadr. 18.
    ,, on horseback, Traj. 1: Hadr. 16: M. Aur. 12: Sev. Alex. 5: Sev. Alex. and Jul. Mam. 5.
    ,, ,, ,, or equestrian statue, Ant. Pius, 1.
    ,, ,, ,, slaying barbarian, Constantine I. 3: Constantius II. 8: Decen. 2.
    ,, presiding at congiarium, Sev. Alex. 3: Gord. III. 12.
    ,, receiving ears of corn from Ceres, Ant. Pius, 16.
    ,, ,, globe from Jupiter, Com. 9: Phil. I.
    ,, ,, globe from Sol, Gord. III. 2.
    ,, ,, olive-branch from Roma, Ant. Pius, 13: L. Ver. 5.
    ,, ,, Palladium from Roma, Com. 32.

Emperor receiving soldiers, Gord. III. 17.
,,   ,,   Victory from Spes, Sev. Alex. 9.
,,   ,,   wreath from Victory, L. Ver. 1 : Com. 6.
,,   sacrificing, Ant. Pius, 23 : Volus. 3.
,,   ,,   and Felicitas, Com. 35 ; 36.
,,   ,,   before Roma, Fortuna, and Victory, Com. 7.
,,   ,,   in view of fleet, Com. 44 ; 45 ; 46.
,,   ,,   to Fortuna, Com. 18.
,,   ,,   to Hercules, Com. 33 ; 34.
,,   ,,   to Jupiter, Com. 3 : Sev. Alex. 6 ; 7 : Sev. Alex. and Jul. Mam. 3 ; 4.
,,   ,,   to Neptune, Com. 30.
,,   ,,   to Roma, Traj. 2 : Sev. Alex. 8 : Gallus and Volus. 1.
,,   ,,   to Sol, Gord. III. 14.
,,   ,,   to Victory, Gord. III. 16.
Emperors crowned by senator and soldier, Gallus and Volus. 1.
,,   holding Victory, Valer. 4.
,,   on horseback, Phil. I. and Phil. II. : Volus. 2 : Gallien. and Salonina, 2 : Gallien. and Saloninus.
,,   presiding at congiarium, Pupien. : Valer. 3 : Valer. and Gallien.
,,   sacrificing, Phil. I., Otacil., and Phil. II. 1.
,,   ,,   to Jupiter, Phil. I., Otacil., and Phil. II. 4.
Euphrates and Tigris, Gord. III. 11 ; 14.

F.

Faustina in character of Diana as Hecate, Faust. Jun. 8.
,,   presenting the Graces to Vesta, Faust. Jun. 7.
Faustina Jun. receiving cornucopiæ from two genii, M. Aur. 11.
Faustina Sen. stepping into biga, Faust. Sen. 4.
Fecunditas ; see Julia Domna.
Felicitas, Traj. 1 : Hadr. 1 : Ant. Pius, 13 : Sev. Alex. and Jul. Mam. 1 ; 2 : Jul. Mam. 1 ; 2 ; 4.
,,   and Pudicitia, Otacil. 1 ; 2.
,,   Roma, Victory, and Emperor, Com. 32.
,,   sacrifice to, Com. 35 ; 36.
Female figure feeding serpent entwined around Salus, M. Aur. 7 ; 8 : Com. 4.

Fides, Gallien. 4.
Figure of City, (Nicomedia?) Constantius II. 2; 3.
Flamines Diales, Sev. Alex. 8.
Flavian Amphitheatre or Colosseum, Sev. Alex. 2: Gord. III. 13.
Fleet entering harbour of Ostia, Com. 44; 45; 46.
Fortuna, Sev. Alex. 8.
,, sacrifice to, Com. 18.
,, statue of, in temple, **Gallus and Volus. 1.**
,, Roma, and Victory, with Emperor at sacrifice, Com. 7.
Fountain of Meta Sudans, Sev. Alex. 2: Gord. III. 13.

G.

Games of the Circus Maximus, Gord. III. 5.
,, of the Flavian Amphitheatre or Colosseum, Gord. III. 13.
Germania, Domit. 1.
Germany, conquest in, Domit. 1: M. Aur. 13; 14.
Gorgons' heads? Gallus, 1; 5: Gallus and Volus. 2.
Graces, group of, Faust. Jun. 7.

H.

Hecate; see Diana.
Hercules, Com. 37; 38: Gallien. 3.
,, crowned by Victory, Ant. Pius, 17: Com. 2.
,, crowning himself, Com. 14.
,, holding branch of apple-tree of Hesperides, Hadr. 5.
,, in Garden of Hesperides, Ant. Pius, 17.
,, in quadriga drawn by Centaurs, M. Aur. 3.
,, leaning on club, Com. 39; 40: Claud. II. 1.
,, ploughing with yoke of oxen, Com. 41; 42.
,, sacrifice to, Com. 33; 34.
,, slaying Nessus, M. Aur. 1.
,, and Bacchus, Sept. Sev. 2.
,, Juno Moneta, and Jupiter, Diocl. 9.

Hesperides, apple-tree of, Ant. Pius, 17.
," branch of apple-tree of, held by Hercules, Hadr. 5.
," Garden of, Ant. Pius, 17.
Hilaritas and Salus, Com. 23.
Hound of Diana Venatrix, Ant. Pius, 9 : Faust. Jun. 1.
," of Silvanus, Ant. Pius, 19 ; 20.

I.

Isis Sothis seated on the Dog, Faust. Jun. 3.
," with peacock and lion, Faust. Jun. 4.
Iulus; see Aeneas.

J.

Julia Domna, as Fecunditas, with Caracalla and Geta, Jul. Dom. 2.
Julia Mamaea, with Felicitas, Jul. Mam. 1 ; 2 ; 4.
,, ,, with Felicitas before Severus Alexander, Sev. Alex. and Jul. Mam. 1 ; 2.
,, ,, with Securitas, Jul. Mam. 3.
Juno, Jupiter, and Minerva, Com. 10.
Juno Martialis, statue of, in temple, Gallus, 1; 5 : Gallus and Volus. 2.
Juno Moneta, Jupiter, and Hercules, Diocl. 9.
Jupiter, Hadr. 2 : Diocl. 1; 2.
," holding circle containing the Seasons, Com. 15.
," in quadriga, Ant. Pius, 24.
," Juvenis, Com. 24.
," presenting globo to Emperor, Com. 9 : Phil. I.
," protecting Marcus Aurelius and Lucius Verus, M. Aur. 10 : L. Ver. 3 ; 4.
," sacrifice to, Com. 3 : Sev. Alex. 6 ; 7 : Sev. Alex. and Jul. Mam. 3 ; 4 : Phil. I., Otacil., and Phil. II. 4.
," seated on Amalthea, Ant. Pius, 18.
," statue of, in temple, Phil. I., Otacil., and Phil. II. 3.
," Juno, and Minerva, Com. 10.
," Juno Moneta, and Hercules, Diocl. 9.
Jupiter Serapis piloting boat, Com. 44 ; 45 ; 46.

L.

Labarum, Constans, 4 : **Valens**, 1 : Honor. 2.
Largitio, Constantius II. 9.
Laurel-wreath, Gallien. 14 : **Constantine II. 2** : Constans, 2 : Constantius II. 4 ; **5.**
Liberalitas, Sev. Alex. 3 : **Pupien.** : Gord. III. 12 : Valer. 3 : Valer. and Gallien.
Libertas, Gallien. **11.**
Lion bearing **Cybele**, Faust. Sen. 1 ; **5** : Lucil. 2.
,, with Africa, **Com. 29.**
,, with Isis Sothis, Faust. Jun. 4.
Lion-hunt, Hadr. 8.
Lituus, Caracal.
Lucifer bearing torch before Sol, Ant. Pius, 7.
Lucilla and Ceres, Lucil. 1.
Lucius Verus and Marcus Aurelius **protected by Jupiter, M. Aur. 10 : L. Ver.**
   3 ; 4.

M.

Marcia ? as Amazon, and Commodus, **Com. 33.**
Marcus Aurelius and Lucius Verus **protected by Jupiter, M. Aur. 10 : L. Ver.**
   3 ; 4.
Mars crowning Caesar, Phil. II.
,, and Roma **conducting triumphal quadriga, Gord. III. 3** : Phil. I., Otacil.,
   and Phil. II. 2.
,, Roma, and Caesar, Phil. II.
,, Gradivus, M. Aur., and Com.
,, Pacator, Com. 25.
Meta Sudans, Sev. Alex. 2 : Gord. III. 13.
,,   ,,   Fountain of ? Sev. Alex. 2 : Gord. III. 13.
Minerva, Domit. 2 ; 4 : Com. 11.
   ,, and Neptune, Ant. Pius, 12.
   ,, ,, **Neptune; contest for** Attica, Hadr. 19.
   ,, ,, Victory, feeding **serpent on altar, M. Aur. 9.**
   ,, Jupiter, and Juno, Com. 10.
   ,, present with Vulcan forging **thunderbolt**, Faust. Sen. 6.

Minerva Propugnatrix (Pallas Promachos) on rostral column, Domit. 3.
„ Victrix, Com. 26 ; 27.
Modius on altar, Hadr. 3.
Moneta ; see Juno Moneta.
Monetæ, Three, Elagab.: **Sev. Alex. 1**: Maximin I. 1: Gord. III. 1; **10**: Gallus, 2; **3**: Volus. 1: Valer. 1; 2: Gallien. 1; 5; 6; 7; 8; 9: Gallien. and Salonina, 3: Salonina, 1; 2: Claud. **II.** 2; 3: Florian.: Prob. 1; 2; 3; 4; 5; 6; **7**: Carus: Num. 2; 3: **Carinus, 1**; **2**: Diocl. 3; 4; 5; 6; 7; 8: Maximian I. **1**; **2**; 3; 4: Constantius **I. 1**; 2: Galer. 1; 2; 3: Constantius II. 10.
Muses **with** Apollo Citharœdus, Hadr. 14.

N.

Neptune before walls of Troy, M. Aur. 6.
„ with Emperor sacrificing, **Com. 30**.
„ and Ceres, Ant. Pius, 21.
„ „ Minerva, Ant. Pius, 12.
„ „ Minerva; contest for Attica, Hadr. 19.
Nessus slain by Hercules, M. Aur. 1.
Nicomedia? figure of, Constantius II. 2 ; 3.

O.

Ostia, harbour of, Com. 44 ; **45** ; 46.
Owl on shield, Hadr. 8.
„ eagle, and peacock, **Hadr. 8.**
Oxen, yoke of, ploughing, **driven by Hercules, Com. 41** ; **42.**

P.

Palladium, **Com. 32.**
Panther, Constantine I. 2.
„ horned and winged, of Diana Lucifera, Ant. Pius, 10.
„ of Bacchus, Sept. Sev. 2.
Parthia and Armenia, conquest of, L. Ver. 2.
Patera, Caracal.

Pax, Gallien. 2 ; 12.
Peacock, Faust. Jun. 5.
,, on sceptre, Hadr. 8.
,, with Juno, Gallus, 5 : Gallus and Volus. 2.
,, with Isis Sothis, Faust. Jun. 4.
,, eagle, and owl, Hadr. 8.
Pelta, Com. 33.
Pharos, Com. 44 ; 45 ; 46.
Phœnix held by Aeternitas, Faust. Sen. 2.
,, presented by Caesar to Emperor, Constantine I. 2.
Pietas, Helena.
Plague in Rome, Ant. Pius, 4 ; 5.
Polyhymnia, Hadr. 14.
Popa, Ant. Pius, 23 : Com. 3 ; 35 ; 36 : Gord. III. 16.
Porticoes, eight, on temple, Phil. I., Otacil., and Phil. II. 1.
Praefericulum, Caracal.
Priapic term, Ant. Pius, 21.
Profectio, M. Aur. 12 : Sev. Alex. 5 : Sev. Alex. and Jul. Mam. 5.
Prow of Annona, Hadr. 3.
Pudicitia, Salonina, 3.
,, and Felicitas, Otacil. 1 ; 2.
Python on tripod before Apollo Citharœdus, M. Aur. 4.

Q.

Quadriga of Hercules, drawn by centaurs as Seasons, M. Aur. 3.
,, ,, Jupiter, Ant. Pius, 24.
,, ,, Sol, Ant. Pius, 7 : Gord. III. 14.
,, ,, Victory, M. Aur. 14.
,, triumphal, Traj. 3 : Com. 19 ; 31.
,, ,, conducted by Mars and Roma, Gord. III. 3 : Phil. I., Otacil., and Phil. II. 2.
,, ,, conducted by Roma, L. Ver. 2 : Com. 1 : Gord. III. 4.
Quiver, bow, and club of Hercules, Com. 43.

R.

Raven with Apollo, M. Aur. 4.
,, ,, figure of Salus, M. Aur. 7 ; 8 : Com. 4.

INDEX IV.

Roma, Sept. Sev. 5: Const. Gal. 2: Constans, 5: Grat. 1; 2: Honor. 1: Attalus.
,, bust of, Constantine I. 6; 7.
,, conducting triumphal quadriga, L. Ver. 2: Com. 1: Gord. III. 4.
,, crowned by Victory, L. Ver. 5.
,, crowning Emperor, Gord. **III. 2.**
,, holding inscribed shield, Sev. Alex. 4.
,, presenting olive-branch to Emperor, Ant. Pius, **13**: **L. Ver. 5.**
,, ,, palladium to Emperor, Com. 32.
,, sacrifice to, Traj. 2: **Sev. Alex. 8.**
,, statue of, within templo, Sev. Alex. **8.**
,, and Constantinopolis, Valentinian I. 1.
,, ,, Mars, conducting triumphal quadriga, **Gord. III.** 3: Phil. I., Otacil., and Phil. II. 2.
,, Constantius II., and Constantinopolis, Constantius II. 9.
,, Felicitas, Victory, and **Emperor, Com. 32.**
,, Fortuna, and **Victory, with Emperor at sacrifice, Com. 7.**
,, Mars, and **Caesar, Phil. II.**

S.

Sacrifice, Ant. Pius, 23: Com. 7: Phil. I., Otacil., and Phil. II. 1: Volus. 3.
,, before fleet, Com. 44; 45; 46.
,, to Felicitas, Com. 35; 36.
,, ,, Fortuna, Com. 18.
,, ,, Hercules, **Com. 33**; 34.
,, ,, Jupiter, Com. 3: Sev. Alex. 6; 7: Sev. Alex. and Jul. Mam. 3; 4: Phil. I., Otacil., and Phil. II. 4.
,, ,, Neptune, Com. 30.
,, ,, Roma, Traj. 2: **Sev. Alex. 8**: Gallus and Volus. **1.**
,, ,, Sol, Gord. III. 14.
,, ,, Vesta, Lucil. **3.**
,, ,, Victory, Gord. III. 16.
,, by Silvanus, Hadr. 11; 12.
Sacrificial instruments, Caracal.
Salus, Gallien. 10.
,, figure of, on table, encircled by serpent, **M. Aur. 7**; 8: **Com. 4.**
,, and Aesculapius, Hadr. 6; 7.

Salus and Hilaritas, Com. 23.
Sarmatia, victory in, Constantine II. 1.
Seasons with attributes, Hadr. 17 : Ant. Pius, 14 ; 22 : Com. and Ann. Ver.: Com. 15 ; 20 ; 21.
,, see Centaurs.
Secespita, Caracal.
Securitas, Faust. Sen. 3 : Com. 28 : Jul. Mam. 3 : Magnen. 1 ; 2.
Serpent of Salus, M. Aur. 7 ; 8 : Com. 4.
,, on altar, M. Aur. 9 : Com. 23.
,, see Aesculapius.
Shield of Minerva, ornamented with temples and figures, Domit. 2 ; 4.
,, ,, Roma, ornamented with Wolf and Twins, Ant. Pius, 13.
,, ,, Venus Genetrix, ornamented with figures of Aeneas, Anchises, and Iulus, Hadr. 13.
,, ,, Virtus, ornamented with Wolf and Twins, Com. 8.
Ship in full sail, Com. 22.
Silvanus, Ant. Pius, 19 ; 20.
,, sacrificing, Hadr. 11 ; 12.
Simpulum, Caracal.
Sol in quadriga, Gord. III. 14.
,, ,, ascending clouds, Ant. Pius, 7.
,, presenting globe to Emperor, Gord. III. 2.
,, sacrifice to, Gord. III. 14.
Soldier crowning Emperor, Phil. I.
Soldiers before Emperor, Gord. III. 17.
Spes presenting Victory to Emperor, Sev. Alex. 9.
Statue? equestrian, of Emperor, Ant. Pius, 1.

T.

Tellus, Ant. Pius, 7.
,, with Seasons, Hadr. 17 : Com. 20 ; 21.
,, ,, ,, and cow, Ant. Pius, 14.
Temple, before which Silvanus sacrifices, Hadr. 11 ; 12.
,, octostyle, Phil. I., Otacil., and Phil. II. 4.
,, surmounted by eight porticoes, Phil. I., Otacil., and Phil. II. 1.
,, of Juno Martialis, circular, Gallus, 1 ; 5 : Gallus and Volus. 2.
,, ,, Jupiter, circular, Phil. I., Otacil., and Phil. II. 3.

Temple of Jupiter, hexastyle, Com. 3.
„   „ Roma, distyle, Sev. Alex. 8.
„   „ Roma, hexastyle, Traj. 2.
„   „ Vesta, circular, Lucil. 3.
„   „ Victory, circular, Gord. III. 16.
Term of Priapus, **Ant. Pius, 21.**
Tessera frumentaria; see Liberalitas.
Tibor, Ant. Pius, 4; 5.
„   welcoming serpent of **Aesculapius,** Ant. Pius, 4; 5.
Tibicen, Traj. 2: Ant. Pius, **23**: **Com. 3**; 7: Phil. I., Otacil., and Phil. II. 4:
    Gallus and Volus. **1**: Volus. **3.**
Tigris and Euphrates, **Gord. III. 11**; 14.
Trireme, Gord. III. 15.
Triumph, **Traj. 3**: L. Ver. 2: Com. **1**; 19; 31: Gord. III. **3**; 4: Phil. I.,
    Otacil., and Phil. II. 2.
Trophy, carried by soldiers, **L. Ver. 2.**
Troy, building of, M. Aur. 6.

V.

Venus holding dove, Faust. Jun. 6.
„   Genetrix, Hadr. 13.
„   Genetrix? with cupids in garden, Faust. Jun. 2.
Verus; see Lucius Verus.
Vesta receiving the Graces from Faustina, Faust. **Jun. 7.**
„   sacrifice **to,** Lucil. 3.
„   statue **of,** within temple, Lucil. 3.
Victimarius, **Traj. 2**: Ant. Pius, 23: Gord. III. 16.
Victory, Com. **5**: Sept. Sev. 4: Const. Gal. **1.**
„   armed, statue of, **Gord. III. 16.**
„   bearing trophy and dragging captive, Valentinian I. 2.
„   conducting Emperor, **Constantius** II. 12.
„   crowning Emperor, **Ant. Pius, 16**: Com. **31**; **32**: Sev. Alex. 4: Sev.
        Alex. and Jul. Mam. **1**; **2**: Gord. III. **3**; 4; 5; 11;
        14; 17: Phil. I., Otacil., and **Phil.** II. 2: Gallien. 13:
        Magnen. 3.
„   „   Hercules, Ant. Pius, 17: Com. 2.
„   „   Roma, L. Ver. 5.

Victory dragging Eastern captive, Constantius II. 13.
    ,, erecting trophy before Africa, Com. 29.
    ,, flying above quadriga, Com. 1.
    ,, held by Emperors, Valer. 4.
    ,, in biga, Ant. Pius, 3.
    ,, ,, quadriga, M. Aur. 14.
    ,, inscribing shield, Com. **16**; **17**: Constans, 6; 7: Constantius II. 11.
    ,, ,, shield on trophy, Ant. Pius, 6: M. Aur. 13.
    ,, preceding Emperor, Sev. Alex. 5: Sev. Alex. and Jul. Mam. 5.
    ,, ,, Emperors, Phil. I. and Phil. II.: Volus. 2: Gallien. and Salonina, 2: Gallien. and Saloninus.
    ,, presenting wreath to Emperor, L. Ver. 1: Com. 6.
    ,, sacrifice to, Gord. III. 16.
    ,, sacrificing bull, Ant. Pius, 15.
    ,, with captive, Magnen. 4: Decen. 1; 3.
    ,, ,, soldiers, Tacit.
    ,, and Constantinopolis, Constantine I. 4.
    ,, ,, Minerva feeding serpent on altar, M. Aur. 9.
    ,, Roma, and Fortuna, with Emperor at sacrifice, Com. 7.
Virtus, Com. 8.
    ,, Jupiter, and Emperor, Phil. I.
Vulcan, forging thunderbolt before Minerva, Faust. Sen. 6.

W.

Wolf and Twins, Constantine I. 6; 7.
    ,, ,, ,, see shield of Roma.
    ,, ,, ,, see shield of Virtus.

Y.

Youth with pedum, &c., Ant. Pius, 8.

Z.

Zodiac signs of the, Ant. Pius, 14.

TABLE OF DATES AND TITLES.

DOMITIAN.

A.V.C.	A.D.	
822	69	CAES.
823	70	PRAET.
824	71	COS.
825	72	COS . DES . II.
826	73	COS . II.
827	74	COS . III.
828	75	COS . IV.
829	76	COS . V.
830	77	COS . VI.
831	78	COS . VI.
832	79	COS . VI . DES . VII.
833	80	COS . VII.
834	81	COS . VII.
834	81	AVG ; TR . P ; COS . VII . DES . VIII ; IMP.
835	82	TR . P . I . II ; COS . VIII . DES . IX ; IMP . II.
836	83	TR . P . II . III ; COS . IX . DES . X ; IMP . II . III . IV . V.
837	84	TR . P . III . IV ; COS . X . DES . XI ; IMP . V . VI . VII.
838	85	TR . P . IV . V ; COS . XI . DES . XII ; IMP . VII . VIII . IX . X . XI.
839	86	TR . P . V . VI ; COS . XII . DES . XIII ; IMP . XI . XII . XIII . XIV.
840	87	TR . P . VI . VII ; COS . XIII . DES . XIV ; IMP . XIV.
841	88	TR . P . VII . VIII ; COS . XIV ; IMP . XIV . XV . XVI.
842	89	TR . P . VIII . IX ; COS . XIV . DES . XV ; IMP . XVII . XVIII . XIX . XX . XXI.

A.V.C.	A.D.	
843	90	AVG; TR.P.IX.X; COS.XV; IMP.XXI.
844	91	TR.P.X.XI; COS.XV.DES.XVI; IMP.XXI.
845	92	TR.P.XI.XII; COS.XVI; IMP.XXI.XXII.
846	93	TR.P.XII.XIII; COS.XVI; IMP.XXII.
847	94	TR.P.XIII.XIV; COS.XVI.DES.XVII; IMP.XXII.
848	95	TR.P.XIV.XV; COS.XVII; IMP.XXII.
849	96	TR.P.XV.XVI; COS.XVII; IMP.XXII.
		PAT.PATR; PONT.MAX. (A.V.C. 834—A.D. 81) GERM.; CENS.PER. (A.V.C. 837—A.D. 84).

TRAJAN.

A.V.C.	A.D.	
844	91	COS.
850	97	CAES; TR.P; COS.DES.II; IMP.
851	98	TR.P.I; COS.II; IMP.
851	98	AVG; TR.P.I.II; COS.II; IMP.
852	99	TR.P.II.III; COS.II.DES.III; IMP.
853	100	TR.P.III.IV; COS.III.DES.IV; IMP.
854	101	TR.P.IV.V; COS.IV; IMP.
855	102	TR.P.V.VI; COS.IV; IMP.II.III.
856	103	TR.P.VI.VII; COS.IV.DES.V; IMP.III.IV.
857	104	TR.P.VII.VIII; COS.V; IMP.IV.
858	105	TR.P.VIII.IX; COS.V; IMP.IV.
859	106	TR.P.IX.X; COS.V; IMP.V.
860	107	TR.P.X.XI; COS.V; IMP.V.
861	108	TR.P.XI.XII; COS.V; IMP.VI.
862	109	TR.P.XII.XIII; COS.V; IMP.VI.
863	110	TR.P.XIII.XIV; COS.V; IMP.VI.
864	111	TR.P.XIV.XV; COS.V.DES.VI; IMP.VI.
865	112	TR.P.XV.XVI; COS.VI; IMP.VI.
866	113	TR.P.XVI.XVII; COS.VI; IMP.VI.
867	114	TR.P.XVII.XVIII; COS.VI; IMP.VI.
868	115	TR.P.XVIII.XIX; COS.VI; IMP.VII.VIII.IX.
869	116	TR.P.XIX.XX; COS.VI; IMP.X.XI.
870	117	TR.P.XX.XXI; COS.VI; IMP.XI.XII.XIII.

A.V.C.	A.D.	
		GERM. (A.V.C. 850—A.D. 97) PONT. MAX. (A.V.C. 851—A.D. 98) PAT. **PATR**; OPT. PRIN. (A.V.C. 852—A.D. 99) **DAC.** (A.V.C. 856—A.D. 103) OPT. AVG. (A.V.C. 867—A.D. 114) PARTH. (A.V.C. 869—A.D. 116).

HADRIAN.

A.V.C.	A.D.	
862	109	COS.
870	117	AVG; TR.P; COS.DES.II; **IMP**.
871	118	TR.P.I.II; COS.II.DES.III; IMP.
872	119	TR.P.II.III; COS.III; IMP.II.
873	120	TR.P.III.IV; COS.III; IMP.II.
874	121	TR.P.IV.V; COS.III; IMP.II.
875	122	TR.P.V.VI; COS.III; IMP.II.
876	123	TR.P.VI.VII; COS.III; IMP.II.
877	124	TR.P.VII.VIII; COS.III; IMP.II.
878	125	TR.P.VIII.IX; COS.III; IMP.II.
879	126	TR.P.IX.X; COS.III; IMP.II.
880	127	TR.P.X.XI; COS.III; IMP.II.
881	128	TR.P.XI.XII; COS.III; IMP.II.
882	129	TR.P.XII.XIII; COS.III; IMP.II.
883	130	TR.P.XIII.XIV; COS.III; IMP.II.
884	131	TR.P.XIV.XV; COS.III; IMP.II.
885	132	TR.P.XV.XVI; COS.III; IMP.II.
886	133	TR.P.XVI.XVII; COS.III; IMP.II.
887	134	TR.P.XVII.XVIII; COS.III; IMP.II.
888	135	TR.P.XVIII.XIX; **COS.III**; IMP.II.
889	136	TR.P.XIX.XX; COS.III; IMP.II.
890	137	TR.P.XX.XXI; COS.III; IMP.II.
891	138	TR.P.XXI; COS.III; IMP.II.
		PONT. MAX; OPT; GERM; DAC; PARTH. (A.V.C. 870—A.D. 117) PAT. PATR. (A.V.C. 870–881—A.D. 117–128).

AELIUS CAESAR.

A.V.C.	A.D.	
889	136	**CAES**; TR.P; COS.DES.II.
890	137	TR.P.I.II; COS.II.
891	138	TR.P.II; COS.II

ANTONINUS PIUS.

A.V.C.	A.D.	
873	120	COS.
891	138	CAES; TR.P; COS; IMP.
891	138	AVG; TR.P; COS.DES.II; IMP.
892	139	TR.P.II; COS.II.DES.III; IMP.II.
893	140	TR.P.III; COS.III; IMP.II.
894	141	TR.P.IV; COS.III; IMP.II.
895	142	TR.P.V; COS.III; IMP.II.
896	143	TR.P.VI; COS.III; IMP.II.
897	144	TR.P.VII; COS.III.DES.IV; IMP.II.
898	145	TR.P.VIII; COS.IV; IMP.II.
899	146	TR.P.IX; COS.IV; IMP.II.
900	147	TR.P.X; COS.IV; IMP.II.
901	148	TR.P.XI; COS.IV; IMP.II.
902	149	TR.P.XII; COS.IV; IMP.II.
903	150	TR.P.XIII; COS.IV; IMP.II.
904	151	TR.P.XIV; COS.IV; IMP.II.
905	152	TR.P.XV; COS.IV; IMP.II.
906	153	TR.P.XVI; COS.IV; IMP.II.
907	154	TR.P.XVII; COS.IV; IMP.II.
908	155	TR.P.XVIII; COS.IV; IMP.II.
909	156	TR.P.XIX; COS.IV; IMP.II.
910	157	TR.P.XX; COS.IV; IMP.II.
911	158	TR.P.XXI; COS.IV; IMP.II.
912	159	TR.P.XXII; COS.IV; IMP.II.
913	160	TR.P.XXIII; COS.IV; IMP.II.
914	161	TR.P.XXIV; COS.IV; IMP.II.

PONT.MAX; PIVS. (A.V.C. 891—A.D. 138) PAT.PATR. (A.V.C. 892—A.D. 139).

MARCUS AURELIUS.

A.V.C.	A.D.	
892	139	CAES; COS.DES.
893	140	COS.
897	144	COS.DES.II.
898	145	COS.II.
900	147	TR.P; COS.II

TABLE OF DATES AND TITLES.

A.V.C.	A.D.	
901	148	CAES; TR.P.II; COS.II.
902	149	TR.P.III; COS.II.
903	150	TR.P.IV; COS.II.
904	151	TR.P.V; COS.II.
905	152	TR.P.VI; COS.II.
906	153	TR.P.VII; COS.II.
907	154	TR.P.VIII; COS.II.
908	155	TR.P.IX; COS.II.
909	156	TR.P.X; COS.II.
910	157	TR.P.XI; COS.II.
911	158	TR.P.XII; COS.II.
912	159	TR.P.XIII; COS.II.
913	160	TR.P.XIV; COS.II.DES.III.
914	161	TR.P.XV; COS.III.
914	161	AVG; TR.P.XV; COS.III; IMP.
915	162	TR.P.XVI; COS.III; IMP.
916	163	TR.P.XVII; COS.III; IMP.II.
917	164	TR.P.XVIII; COS.III; IMP.II.
918	165	TR.P.XIX; COS.III; IMP.II.III.
919	166	TR.P.XX; COS.III; IMP.III.IV.
920	167	TR.P.XXI; COS.III; IMP.IV.
921	168	TR.P.XXII; COS.III; IMP.IV.V.
922	169	TR.P.XXIII; COS.III; IMP.V.
923	170	TR.P.XXIV; COS.III; IMP.V.
924	171	TR.P.XXV; COS.III; IMP.VI.
925	172	TR.P.XXVI; COS.III; IMP.VI.
926	173	TR.P.XXVII; COS.III; IMP.VI.
927	174	TR.P.XXVIII; COS.III; IMP.VI.VII.
928	175	TR.P.XXIX; COS.III; IMP.VII.VIII.
929	176	TR.P.XXX; COS.III; IMP.VIII.
930	177	TR.P.XXXI; COS.III; IMP.VIII.IX.
931	178	TR.P.XXXII; COS.III; IMP.IX.
932	179	TR.P.XXXIII; COS.III; IMP.IX.X.
933	180	TR.P.XXXIV; COS.III; IMP.X.

PONT.MAX. (A.V.C. 914—A.D. 161) ARM. (A.V.C. 917—A.D. 164) PARTH.MAX; MED; **PAT.PATR.** (A.V.C. 919—A.D. 166) GERM. (A.V.C. 925—A.D. 172) SARM. (A.V.C. **928**—A.D. 175).

LUCIUS VERUS.

A.V.C.	A.D.	
906	153	COS. DES.
907	154	COS.
913	160	COS. DES. II.
914	161	COS. II.
914	161	AVG; TR. P; COS. II; IMP.
915	162	TR. P. II; COS. II; IMP.
916	163	TR. P. III; COS. II; IMP. II.
917	164	TR. P. IV; COS. II; IMP. II.
918	165	TR. P. V; COS. II; IMP. II. III.
919	166	TR. P. VI; COS. II. DES. III; IMP. III. IV.
920	167	TR. P. VII; COS. III; IMP. IV.
921	168	TR. P. VIII; COS. III; IMP. IV. V.
922	169	TR. P. IX; COS. III; IMP. V.

ARM. (A.V.C. 916—A.D. 163) PARTH. MAX. (A.V.C. 918—A.D. 165) MED; PAT. PATR. (A.V.C. 919—A.D. 166).

COMMODUS.

A.V.C.	A.D.	
919-927	166-174	CAES.
928	175	COS. DES.
929	176	TR. P; COS. DES; IMP.
930	177	TR. P. I. II; COS; IMP.
930	177	AVG; TR. P. II; COS; IMP. I. II.
931	178	TR. P. III; COS. DES. II; IMP. II.
932	179	TR. P. IV; COS. II; IMP. II. III.
933	180	TR. P. V; COS. II. DES. III; IMP. III. IV.
934	181	TR. P. VI; COS. III; IMP. IV.
935	182	TR. P. VII; COS. III. DES. IV; IMP. IV. V.
936	183	TR. P. VIII; COS. IV; IMP. V. VI.
937	184	TR. P. IX; COS. IV; IMP. VI. VII.
938	185	TR. P. X; COS. IV. DES. V; IMP. VII.
939	186	TR. P. XI; COS. V; IMP. VII. VIII.
940	187	TR. P. XII; COS. V; IMP. VIII.
941	188	TR. P. XIII; COS. V; IMP. VIII.
942	189	TR. P. XIV; COS. V; DES. VI; IMP. VIII.

TABLE OF DATES AND TITLES.

A.V.C.	A.D.	
943	190	AVG; TR.P.XV; COS.VI; IMP.VIII.
944	191	TR.P.XVI; COS.VI.DES.VII; IMP.VIII.
945	192	TR.P.XVII.XVIII; COS.VII; IMP.VIII.

GERM. (A.V.C. 925—A.D. 172) PRINC.IVV; SARM. (A.V.C. 928—A.D. 175) PAT. PATR. (A.V.C. 930—A.D. 177) PIVS; PONT.MAX. (A.V.C. 936—A.D. 183) BRIT. (A.V.C. 937—A.D. 184) FEL. (A.V.C. 938—A.D. 185).

SEPTIMIUS SEVERUS.

A.V.C.	A.D.	
938	185	COS.
946	193	AVG; TR.P; COS.DES.II; IMP.
947	194	TR.P.II; COS.II; IMP.I.II.III.IV.
948	195	TR.P.III; COS.II; IMP.IV.V.VI.VII.
949	196	TR.P.IV; COS.II; IMP.VII.VIII.
950	197	TR.P.V; COS.II; IMP.VIII.IX.X.
951	198	TR.P.VI; COS.II; IMP.X.XI.
952	199	TR.P.VII; COS.II; IMP.XI.
953	200	TR.P.VIII; COS.II; IMP.XI.
954	201	TR.P.IX; COS.II.DES.III; IMP.XI.
955	202	TR.P.X; COS.III; IMP.XI.
956	203	TR.P.XI; COS.III; IMP.XI.
957	204	TR.P.XII; COS.III; IMP.XI.
958	205	TR.P.XIII; COS.III; IMP.XI.
959	206	TR.P.XIV; COS.III; IMP.XI.
960	207	TR.P.XV; COS.III; IMP.XII.
961	208	TR.P.XVI; COS.III; IMP.XII.
962	209	TR.P.XVII; COS.III; IMP.XII.
963	210	TR.P.XVIII; COS.III; IMP.XII.
964	211	TR.P.XIX; COS.III; IMP.XII.

PONT.MAX; PAT.PATR; OPT.PRINC. (A.V.C. 947—A.D. 194) PIVS; ARAB; ADIAB; PARTH. (A.V.C. 948—A.D. 195) PARTH.MAX. (A.V.C. 951—A.D. 198) BRIT. (A.V.C. 963—A.D. 210).

CARACALLA.

A.V.C.	A.D.	
949	196	CAES.
950	197	IMP.
951	198	IMP.
951	198	AVG; TR.P; IMP.
952	199	TR.P.II; IMP.
953	200	TR.P.III; IMP.
954	201	TR.P.IV; COS.DES; IMP.
955	202	TR.P.V; COS; IMP.
956	203	TR.P.VI; COS; IMP.
957	204	TR.P.VII; COS.DES.II; IMP.
958	205	TR.P.VIII; COS.II; IMP.
959	206	TR.P.IX; COS.II; IMP.
960	207	TR.P.X; COS.II.DES.III; IMP.
961	208	TR.P.XI; COS.III; IMP.II.
962	209	TR.P.XII; COS.III; IMP.II.
963	210	TR.P.XIII; COS.III; IMP.II.
964	211	TR.P.XIV; COS.III; IMP.II.
965	212	TR.P.XV; COS.III.DES.IV; IMP.II.
966	213	TR.P.XVI; COS.IV; IMP.II.
967	214	TR.P.XVII; COS.IV; IMP.III.
968	215	TR.P.XVIII; COS.IV; IMP.III.
969	216	TR.P.XIX; COS.IV; IMP.III.
970	217	TR.P.XX; COS.IV; IMP.III.

PRINC.IVV. (A.V.C. 949—A.D. 196) PONT. (A.V.C. 950—A.D. 197) PARTH.MAX. (A.V.C. 951—A.D. 198) PIVS. (A.V.C. 954—A.D. 201) BRIT. (A.V.C. 963—A.D. 210) PAT.PATR; PONT.MAX. (A.V.C. 964—A.D. 211) GERM. (A.V.C. 966—A.D. 213).

GETA.

A.V.C.	A.D.	
951-954	198-201	CAES.
955	202	COS.DES.
956-959	203-206	COS.
960	207	COS.DES.II.
961	208	COS.II.
962	209	AVG; TR.P; COS.II.

A.V.C.	A.D.	
963	210	AVG; TR.P.II; COS.II.
964	211	TR.P.III; COS.II.
965	212	TR.P.IV; COS.II.

PRINC.IVV; PONT. (A.V.C. 951—A.D. 198) PIVS. (A.V.C. 962—A.D. 209) BRIT. (A.V.C. 963—A.D. 210) PAT. PATR. (A.V.C. 964—A.D. 211).

ELAGABALUS.

A.V.C.	A.D.	
971	218	AVG; TR.P; COS.DES.II.
972	219	TR.P.II; COS.II.DES.III.
973	220	TR.P.III; COS.III.
974	221	TR.P.IV; COS.III.DES.IV.
975	222	TR.P.V; COS.IV.

PAT.PATR; PONT.MAX; PIVS; FEL. (A.V.C. 971—A.D. 218).

SEVERUS ALEXANDER.

A.V.C.	A.D.	
974	221	CAES; COS.DES.
975	222	COS.
975	222	AVG; TR.P; COS.
976	223	TR.P.II; COS.
977	224	TR.P.III; COS.
978	225	TR.P.IV; COS.DES.II.
979	226	TR.P.V; COS.II.
980	227	TR.P.VI; COS.II.
981	228	TR.P.VII; COS.II.DES.III.
982	229	TR.P.VIII; COS.III.
983	230	TR.P.IX; COS.III.
984	231	TR.P.X; COS.III.
985	232	TR.P.XI; COS.III.
986	233	TR.P.XII; COS.III.
987	234	TR.P.XIII; COS.III.
988	235	TR.P.XIV; COS.III.

PRINC.IVV; PONT. (A.V.C. 974—A.D. 221) PAT.PATR. PONT.MAX. (A.V.C. 975—A.D. 222).

MAXIMINUS I.

A.V.C.	A.D.	
988	235	AVG; TR.P; COS.DES.
989	236	TR.P.II; COS.
990	237	TR.P.III; COS.
991	238	TR.P.IV; COS.

PAT.PATR; PONT.MAX; PIVS. (a.v.c. 988—a.d. 235) GERM. (a.v.c. 989—a.d. 236).

PUPIENUS.

991	238	AVG; TR.P; COS.II.

PONT.MAX; PAT.PATR. (a.v.c. 991—a.d. 238).

GORDIAN III.

991	238	CAES.
991	238	AVG; TR.P; COS.DES.
992	239	TR.P.II; COS.
993	240	TR.P.III; COS.DES.II.
994	241	TR.P.IV; COS.II.
995	242	TR.P.V; COS.II.
996	243	TR.P.VI; COS.II.
997	244	TR.P.VII; COS.II.

PRINC.IVV; PAT.PATR; PONT..MAX. (a.v.c. 991—a.d. 238) *PIVS; FEL. (a.v.c. 992—a.d. 239).

PHILIP I.

997	244	AVG; TR.P; COS.DES.
998	245	TR.P.II; COS.
999	246	TR.P.III; COS.DES.II.
1000	247	TR.P.IV; COS.II.DES.III.
1001	248	TR.P.V; COS.III.
1002	249	TR.P.VI; COS.III.

PAT.PATR; PONT.MAX. (a.v.c. 997—a.d. 244) GERM. MAX; CARP.MAX. (a.v.c. 1001—a.d. 248).

* This title occurs on the coins of almost all the subsequent Emperors.

PHILIP II.

A.V.C.	A.D.	
997-998	244-245	CAES.
999	246	COS. DES.
1000	247	AVG; TR.P; COS.DES.II.
1001	248	TR.P.II; COS.II.
1002	249	TR.P.III; COS.II.

PRINC.IVV. (A.V.C. 997—A.D. 244) PAT.PATR; PONT. MAX. (A.V.C. 1000—A.D. 247) GERM.MAX; CARP.MAX. (A.V.C. 1001—A.D. 248).

GALLUS.

1004	251	AVG; TR.P; COS.DES.II.
1005	252	TR.P.II; COS.II.
1006	253	TR.P.III; COS.II.
1007	254	TR.P.IV; COS.II.

PAT.PATR; PONT.MAX. (A.V.C. 1004—A.D. 251).

VOLUSIAN.

1004	251	CAES; TR.P; COS.DES.
1005	252	AVG; TR.P.II; COS.DES.II.
1006	253	TR.P.III; COS.II.
1007	254	TR.P.IV; COS.II.

PRINC.IVV. (A.V.C. 1004—A.D. 251) PAT.PATR; PONT. MAX. (A.V.C. 1005—A.D. 252).

VALERIAN.

1006	253	AVG; TR.P; COS.DES.II.
1007	254	TR.P.II; COS.II.DES.III.
1008	255	TR.P.III; COS.III.
1009	256	TR.P.IV; COS.III.DES.IV.
1010	257	TR.P.V; COS.IV.
1011	258	TR.P.VI; COS.IV.

A.V.C.	A.D.	
1012	259	AVG; TR.P.VII; COS.IV.
1013	260	TR.P.VIII; COS.IV.
		PAT.PATR; PONT.MAX. (A.V.C. 1006—A.D. 253) GERM. MAX. (A.V.C. 1009—A.D. 256).

GALLIENUS.

A.V.C.	A.D.	
1006	253	AVG; TR.P; COS.DES.
1007	254	TR.P.II; COS.DES.II.
1008	255	TR.P.III; COS.II.
1009	256	TR.P.IV; COS.II.DES.III.
1010	257	TR.P.V; COS.III; IMP.III.
1011	258	TR.P.VI; COS.III.
1012	259	TR.P.VII; COS.III.
1013	260	TR.P.VIII; COS.III.DES.IV.
1014	261	TR.P.IX; COS.IV.DES.V.
1015	262	TR.P.X; COS.V.
1016	263	TR.P.XI; COS.V.DES.VI.
1017	264	TR.P.XII; COS.VI.
1018	265	TR.P.XIII; COS.VI.DES.VII.
1019	266	TR.P.XIV; COS.VII.
1020	267	TR.P.XV; COS.VII.
1021	268	TR.P.XVI; COS.VII.
		PAT.PATR; PONT.MAX. (A.V.C. 1006—A.D. 253) GERM. MAX. (A.V.C. 1009—A.D. 256).

SALONINUS.

1006-1009	253-256	CAES.
1010-1013	257-260	AVG.
		PRINC.IVV. (A.V.C. 1006—A.D. 253).

CLAUDIUS II.

A.V.C.	A.D.	
1021	268	AVG; TR.P; COS.DES.II.
1022	269	TR.P.II; COS.II.
1023	270	TR.P.III; COS.II.
		PAT.PATR; PONT.MAX; GERM. (A.V.C. 1021—A.D. 268) GOTHIC. (A.V.C. 1023—A.D. 270).

TACITUS.

A.V.C.	A.D.	
1026	273	COS.
1028	275	AVG; TR.P; COS.DES.II.
1029	276	TR.P.II; COS.II.
		PAT.PATR; PONT.MAX. (A.V.C. 1028—A.D. 275).

FLORIANUS.

1029	276	AVG.
		PRINC.IVV. (A.V.C. 1029—A.D. 276).

PROBUS.

1029	276	AVG; TR.P; COS.DES.
1030	277	TR.P.II; COS.DES.II.
1031	278	TR.P.III; COS.II.DES.III.
1032	279	TR.P.IV; COS.III.
1033	280	TR.P.V; COS.III.DES.IV.
1034	281	TR.P.VI; COS.IV.DES.V.
1035	282	TR.P.VII; COS.V.
		PRINC.IVV; PAT.PATR; PONT.MAX. (A.V.C. 1029—A.D. 276).

CARUS.

1035	282	AVG; TR.P; COS.DES.II.
1036	283	TR.P.II; COS.II.
		PAT.PATR; PONT.MAX. (A.V.C. 1035—A.D. 282).

NUMERIAN.

1035	282	CAES.
1036	283	IMP.
1036	283	AVG; TR.P; COS.DES.
1037	284	TR.P.II; COS.
		PRINC.IVV. (A.V.C. 1035—A.D. 282) PAT.PATR; PONT.MAX. (A.V.C. 1036—A.D. 283).

CARINUS.

A.V.C.	A.D.	
1035	282	CAES; COS.DES.
1036	283	COS; IMP.
1036	283	AVG; TR.P; COS.DES.II.
1037	284	TR.P.II; COS.II.DES.III.
1038	285	TR.P.III.

PRINC.IVV. (A.V.C. 1035—A.D. 282) PAT.PATR; PONT. MAX. (A.V.C. 1036—A.D. 283).

DIOCLETIAN.

1037	284	AVG; TR.P; COS.
1038	285	TR.P.I.II; COS.II.
1039	286	TR.P.II.III; COS.II.DES.III.
1040	287	TR.P.III.IV; COS.III.
1041	288	TR.P.IV.V; COS.III.
1042	289	TR.P.V.VI; COS.III.DES.IV.
1043	290	TR.P.VI.VII; COS.IV.
1044	291	TR.P.VII.VIII; COS.IV.
1045	292	TR.P.VIII.IX; COS.IV.DES.V.
1046	293	TR.P.IX.X; COS.V.
1047	294	TR.P.X.XI; COS.V.
1048	295	TR.P.XI.XII; COS.V.DES.VI; IMP.X.
1049	296	TR.P.XII.XIII; COS.VI.
1050	297	TR.P.XIII.XIV; COS.VI.
1051	298	TR.P.XIV.XV; COS.VI.DES.VII.
1052	299	TR.P.XV.XVI; COS.VII.
1053	300	TR.P.XVI.XVII; COS.VII.
1054	301	TR.P.XVII.XVIII; COS.VII; IMP.XVIII.
1055	302	TR.P.XVIII.XIX; COS.VII.DES.VIII.
1056	303	TR.P.XIX.XX; COS.VIII.DES.IX.
1057	304	TR.P.XX.XXI; COS.IX.
1058	305	TR.P.XXI.XXII; COS.IX.

PAT.PATR; PONT.MAX. (A.V.C. 1037—A.D. 284).

MAXIMIAN.

A.V.C.	A.D.	
1038	285	CAES; TR.P.
1039	286	AVG; TR.P.I.II; COS.DES.
1040	287	TR.P.II.III; COS.DES.II.
1041	288	TR.P.III.IV; COS.II.
1042	289	TR.P.IV.V; COS.II.DES.III.
1043	290	TR.P.V.VI; COS.III.
1044	291	TR.P.VI.VII; COS.III.
1045	292	TR.P.VII.VIII; COS.III.DES.IV.
1046	293	TR.P.VIII.IX; COS.IV; IMP.VIII.
1047	294	TR.P.IX.X; COS.IV.
1048	295	TR.P.X.XI; COS.IV; IMP.VIII.
1049	296	TR.P.XI.XII; COS.IV.DES.V.
1050	297	TR.P.XII.XIII; COS.V.
1051	298	TR.P.XIII.XIV; COS.V.DES.VI.
1052	299	TR.P.XIV.XV; COS.VI.
1053	300	TR.P.XV.XVI; COS.VI.
1054	301	TR.P.XVI.XVII; COS.VI; IMP.XVII.
1055	302	TR.P.XVII.XVIII; COS.VI.DES.VII.
1056	303	TR.P.XVIII.XIX; COS.VII.DES.VIII.
1057	304	TR.P.XIX.XX; COS.VIII.
1058	305	TR.P.XX.XXI; COS.VIII.
1059	306	* * * * * * *
1060	307	COS.IX.DES.X.
1061	308	COS.X.
1062	309	COS.X.
1063	310	COS.X.

PAT.PATR; PONT.MAX. (A.V.C. 1039—A.D. 286) SEN. (A.V.C. 1060—A.D. 307).

CONSTANTIUS I.

1045	292	CAES; TR.P.
1046	293	TR.P.I.II.
1047	294	TR.P.II.III; COS.
1048	295	TR.P.III.IV.COS.DES.II.

TABLE OF DATES AND TITLES.

A.V.C.	A.D.	
1049	296	CAES; TR.P.IV.V; COS.II.
1050	297	TR.P.V.VI; COS.II.
1051	298	TR.P.VI.VII; COS.II.
1052	299	TR.P.VII.VIII; COS.II.DES.III.
1053	300	TR.P.VIII.IX; COS.III.
1054	301	TR.P.IX.X; COS.III.DES.IV.
1055	302	TR.P.X.XI; COS.IV.
1056	303	TR.P.XI.XII; COS.IV.
1057	304	TR.P.XII.XIII; COS.IV.DES.V.
1058	305	AVG; TR.P.XIII.XIV; COS.V.DES.VI.
1059	306	TR.P.XIV.XV; COS.VI.

PRINC.IVV. (A.V.C. 1045—A.D. 292) PAT.PATR; PONT.MAX. (A.V.C. 1058—A.D. 305).

GALERIUS.

1045	292	CAES; TR.P.
1046	293	TR.P.I.II.
1047	294	TR.P.II.III; COS.
1048	295	TR.P.III.IV; COS.
1049	296	TR.P.IV.V; COS.DES.II.
1050	297	TR.P.V.VI; COS.II.
1051	298	TR.P.VI.VII; COS.II.
1052	299	TR.P.VII.VIII; COS.II.DES.III.
1053	300	TR.P.VIII.IX; COS.III.
1054	301	TR.P.IX.X; COS.III.DES.IV.
1055	302	TR.P.X.XI; COS.IV.
1056	303	TR.P.XI.XII; COS.IV.
1057	304	TR.P.XII.XIII; COS.IV.DES.V.
1058	305	AVG; TR.P.XIII.XIV; COS.V.DES.VI.
1059	306	TR.P.XIV.XV; COS.VI.
1060	307	TR.P.XV.XVI; COS.VI.DES.VII.
1061	308	TR.P.XVI.XVII; COS.VII.
1062	309	TR.P.XVII.XVIII; COS.VII.
1063	310	TR.P.XVIII.XIX; COS.VII.DES.VIII.
1064	311	TR.P.XIX.XX; COS.VIII; IMP.XIX.

PRINC.IVV. (A.V.C. 1045—A.D. 292) PAT.PATR; PONT.MAX. (A.V.C. 1058—A.D. 305).

CONSTANTINE THE GREAT.

A.V.C.	A.D.	
1059	306	CAES; TR.P.
1060	307	AVG; TR.P.II; COS.
1061	308	TR.P.III; COS.
1062	309	TR.P.IV; COS.
1063	310	TR.P.V; COS.
1064	311	TR.P.VI; COS.DES.II; IMP.V.
1065	312	TR.P.VII; COS.II.DES.III.
1066	313	TR.P.VIII; COS.III.
1067	314	TR.P.IX; COS.III.DES.IV.
1068	315	TR.P.X; COS.IV; IMP.IX.
1069	316	TR.P.XI; COS.IV.
1070	317	TR.P.XII; COS.IV.
1071	318	TR.P.XIII; COS.IV.DES.V.
1072	319	TR.P.XIV; COS.V.DES.VI; IMP.XIII.
1073	320	TR.P.XV; COS.VI.
1074	321	TR.P.XVI; COS.VI.
1075	322	TR.P.XVII; COS.VI.
1076	323	TR.P.XVIII; COS.VI.
1077	324	TR.P.XIX; COS.VI.
1078	325	TR.P.XX; COS.VI.DES.VII.
1079	326	TR.P.XXI; COS.VII.
1080	327	TR.P.XXII; COS.VII.
1081	328	TR.P.XXIII; COS.VII.DES.VIII; IMP.XXII.
1082	329	TR.P.XXIV; COS.VIII.
1083	330	TR.P.XXV; COS.VIII.
1084	331	TR.P.XXVI; COS.VIII.
1085	332	TR.P.XXVII; COS.VIII.
1086	333	TR.P.XXVIII; COS.VIII.
1087	334	TR.P.XXIX; COS.VIII.
1088	335	TR.P.XXX; COS.VIII.
1089	336	TR.P.XXXI; COS.VIII.
1090	337	TR.P.XXXII; COS.VIII.

PRINC.IVV. (A.V.C. 1059—A.D. 306) PAT.PATR; PONT.MAX. (A.V.C. 1060-1073—A.D. 307-320).

CONSTANTINE II.

A.V.C.	A.D.	
1070	317	CAES.
1073	320	COS.
1074	321	COS. II.
1075	324	COS. III.
1076	329	COS. IV.
1090–1093	337–340	AVG.

PRINC. IVV. (A.V.C. 1070—A.D. 317).

CONSTANS.

1086	333	CAES.
1090	337	AVG.
1092	339	COS.
1095	342	COS. II.
1099–1103	346–350	COS. III.

PRINC. IVV. (A.V.C. 1086—A.D. 333).

CONSTANTIUS II.

1076	323	CAES. TR. P.
1077	324	TR. P. II.
1078	325	TR. P. III.
1079	326	TR. P. IV; COS. I.
1080	327	TR. P. V.
1081	328	TR. P. VI.
1082	329	TR. P. VII.
1083	330	TR. P. VIII.
1084	331	TR. P. IX.
1085	332	TR. P. X.
1086	333	TR. P. XI.
1087	334	TR. P. XII.
1088	335	TR. P. XIII.
1089	336	TR. P. XIV.
1090	337	AVG; TR. P. XV.
1091	338	TR. P. XVI.
1092	339	TR. P. XVII; COS. II.

1093	340	AVG; TR.P.XVIII.
1094	341	TR.P.XIX.
1095	342	TR.P.XX; COS.III.
1096	343	TR.P.XXI.
1097	344	TR.P.XXII.
1098	345	TR.P.XXIII.
1099	346	TR.P.XXIV; COS.IV.
1100	347	TR.P.XXV.
1101	348	TR.P.XXVI.
1102	349	TR.P.XXVII.
1103	350	TR.P.XXVIII.
1104	351	TR.P.XXIX.
1105	352	TR.P.XXX; COS.V.
1106	353	TR.P.XXXI; COS.VI.
1107	354	TR.P.XXXII; COS.VII; IMP.XXX.
1108	355	TR.P.XXXIII.
1109	356	TR.P.XXXIV; COS.VIII.
1110	357	TR.P.XXXV; COS.IX.
1111	358	TR.P.XXXVI.
1112	359	TR.P.XXXVII.
1113	360	TR.P.XXXVIII; COS.X.
1114	361	TR.P.XXXIX.

PRINC.IVV. (a.v.c. 1076—a.d. 323).

MAGNENTIUS.

1103-1106	350-353	AVG.

DECENTIUS.

1104	351	CAES.
1105-1106	352-353	COS.

CONSTANTIUS GALLUS.

1104	351	CAES.
1105	352	COS.
1106	353	COS.II.
1107	354	COS.III.

JULIAN II.

A.V.C.	A.D.	
1108	355	CAES.
1109	356	COS.
1110	357	COS. II.
1113	360	COS. III.
1113	360	AVG; COS. III.
1114	362	COS. III. IMP. VII.
1115	363	COS. IV. IMP. VII.

PRINC. IVV. (A.V.C. 1108—A.D. 355) PAT. PATR; PONT. MAX. (A.V.C. 1113—A.D. 360).

VALENTINIAN I.

A.V.C.	A.D.	
1117	364	AVG.
1118	365	COS.
1121	368	COS. II.
1122	369	COS. II; IMP. VI.
1123	370	COS. III.
1126	373	COS. IV.
1128	375	COS. IV.

PAT. PATR; PONT. MAX. (A.V.C. 1117—A.D. 364).

VALENS.

A.V.C.	A.D.	
1117	364	AVG.
1118	365	COS.
1121	368	COS. II.
1122	369	COS. II. IMP. VI.
1123	370	COS. III.
1126	373	COS. IV.
1129	376	COS. V.
1131	378	COS. VI.

PAT. PATR; PONT. MAX. (A.V.C. 1117—A.D. 364).

GRATIAN.

A.V.C.	A.D.	
1119	366	COS.
1120	367	AVG.
1122	369	COS; IMP. II.
1124	371	COS. II.
1127	374	COS. III.
1130	377	COS. IV.
1133	380	COS. V.
1136	383	COS. V.

PAT. PATR; PONT. MAX. (A.V.C. 1120—A.D. 367).

HONORIUS.

A.V.C.	A.D.	
1139	386	CAES; COS.
1146	393	AVG.
1147	394	COS. II.
1149	396	COS. III.
1151	398	COS. IV.
1155	402	COS. V.
1157	404	COS. VI.
1160	407	COS. VII.
1162	409	COS. VIII.
1165	412	COS. IX.
1168	415	COS. X.
1170	417	COS. XI.
1171	418	COS. XII.
1175	422	COS. XIII.
1176	423	COS. XIII.

PRISCUS ATTALUS.

A.V.C.	A.D.	
1162	409	} AVG.
1163	410	
1167	414	} AVG.
1169	416	

TABLE
OF THE
RELATIVE WEIGHTS OF ENGLISH GRAINS AND FRENCH GRAMMES.

Grains.	Grammes.	Grains.	Grammes.	Grains.	Grammes.	Grains.	Grammes.
1	·064	41	2·656	81	5·248	121	7·840
2	·129	42	2·720	82	5·312	122	7·905
3	·194	43	2·785	83	5·378	123	7·970
4	·259	44	2·850	84	5·442	124	8·035
5	·324	45	2·915	85	5·508	125	8·100
6	·388	46	2·980	86	5·572	126	8·164
7	·453	47	3·045	87	5·637	127	8·229
8	·518	48	3·110	88	5·702	128	8·294
9	·583	49	3·175	89	5·767	129	8·359
10	·648	50	3·240	90	5·832	130	8·424
11	·712	51	3·304	91	5·896	131	8·488
12	·777	52	3·368	92	5·961	132	8·553
13	·842	53	3·434	93	6·026	133	8·618
14	·907	54	3·498	94	6·091	134	8·682
15	·972	55	3·564	95	6·156	135	8·747
16	1·036	56	3·628	96	6·220	136	8·812
17	1·101	57	3·693	97	6·285	137	8·877
18	1·166	58	3·758	98	6·350	138	8·942
19	1·231	59	3·823	99	6·415	139	9·007
20	1·296	60	3·888	100	6·480	140	9·072
21	1·360	61	3·952	101	6·544	141	9·136
22	1·425	62	4·017	102	6·609	142	9·200
23	1·490	63	4·082	103	6·674	143	9·265
24	1·555	64	4·146	104	6·739	144	9·330
25	1·620	65	4·211	105	6·804	145	9·395
26	1·684	66	4·276	106	6·868	146	9·460
27	1·749	67	4·341	107	6·933	147	9·525
28	1·814	68	4·406	108	6·998	148	9·590
29	1·879	69	4·471	109	7·063	149	9·655
30	1·944	70	4·536	110	7·128	150	9·720
31	2·008	71	4·600	111	7·192	151	9·784
32	2·073	72	4·665	112	7·257	152	9·848
33	2·138	73	4·729	113	7·322	153	9·914
34	2·202	74	4·794	114	7·387	154	9·978
35	2·267	75	4·859	115	7·452	155	10·044
36	2·332	76	4·924	116	7·516	156	10·108
37	2·397	77	4·989	117	7·581	157	10·173
38	2·462	78	5·054	118	7·646	158	10·238
39	2·527	79	5·119	119	7·711	159	10·303
40	2·592	80	5·184	120	7·776	160	10·368

TABLE

OF THE
RELATIVE WEIGHTS OF ENGLISH GRAINS AND FRENCH GRAMMES.

Grains.	Grammes.	Grains.	Grammes.	Grains.	Grammes.	Grains.	Grammes.
161	10·432	201	13·024	241	15·616	290	18·79
162	10·497	202	13·089	242	15·680	300	19·44
163	10·562	203	13·154	243	15·745	310	20·08
164	10·626	204	13·219	244	15·810	320	20·73
165	10·691	205	13·284	245	15·875	330	21·38
166	10·756	206	13·348	246	15·940	340	22·02
167	10·821	207	13·413	247	16·005	350	22·67
168	10·886	208	13·478	248	16·070	360	23·32
169	10·951	209	13·543	249	16·135	370	23·97
170	11·016	210	13·608	250	16·200	380	24·62
171	11·080	211	13·672	251	16·264	390	25·27
172	11·145	212	13·737	252	16·328	400	25·92
173	11·209	213	13·802	253	16·394	410	26·56
174	11·274	214	13·867	254	16·458	420	27·20
175	11·339	215	13·932	255	16·524	430	27·85
176	11·404	216	13·996	256	16·588	440	28·50
177	11·469	217	14·061	257	16·653	450	29·15
178	11·534	218	14·126	258	16·718	460	29·80
179	11·599	219	14·191	259	16·783	470	30·45
180	11·664	220	14·256	260	16·848	480	31·10
181	11·728	221	14·320	261	16·912	490	31·75
182	11·792	222	14·385	262	16·977	500	32·40
183	11·858	223	14·450	263	17·042	510	33·04
184	11·922	224	14·515	264	17·106	520	33·68
185	11·988	225	14·580	265	17·171	530	34·34
186	12·052	226	14·644	266	17·236	540	34·98
187	12·117	227	14·709	267	17·301	550	35·64
188	12·182	228	14·774	268	17·366	560	36·28
189	12·247	229	14·839	269	17·431	570	36·93
190	12·312	230	14·904	270	17·496	580	37·58
191	12·376	231	14·968	271	17·560	590	38·23
192	12·441	232	15·033	272	17·625	600	38·88
193	12·506	233	15·098	273	17·689	700	45·36
194	12·571	234	15·162	274	17·754	800	51·84
195	12·636	235	15·227	275	17·819	900	58·32
196	12·700	236	15·292	276	17·884	1000	64·80
197	12·765	237	15·357	277	17·949	2000	129·60
198	12·830	238	15·422	278	18·014	3000	194·40
199	12·895	239	15·487	279	18·079	4000	259·20
200	12·960	240	15·552	280	18·144	5000	324·00

TABLE

FOR

CONVERTING ENGLISH INCHES INTO MILLIMÈTRES AND THE MEASURES OF MIONNET'S SCALE.

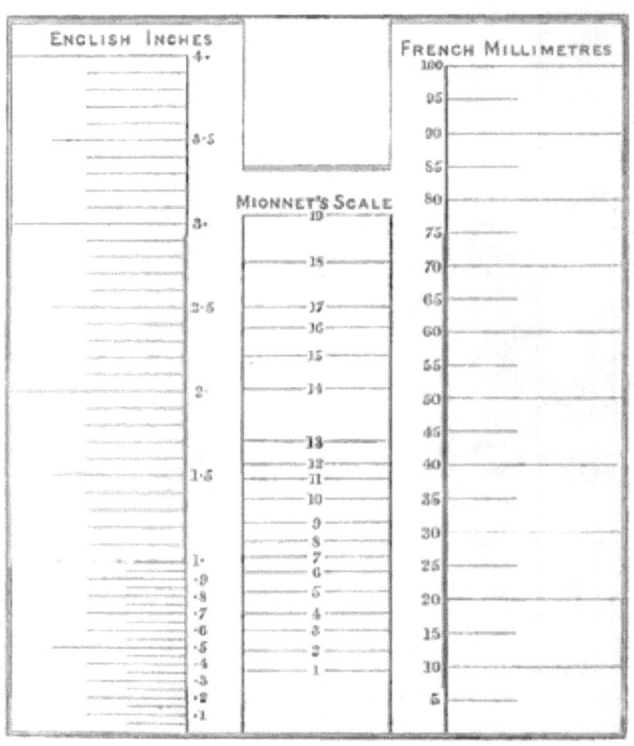

PL II

Autotype, London

Pl. IV

Autotype, London

PL. V

AUTOTYPE, LONDON.

Autotype, London

Mary Godsall del. Autotype, London

PL. VIII

Autotype, London.

PL X

MARY GOOSALL DEL.　　　　　　　　　AUTOTYPE LONDON.

PL. XII

AUTOTYPE, LONDON

MARY GOODSALL DEL.   AUTOTYPE, LONDON

PL. XIV

AUTOTYPE, LONDON.

Mary Godsall del.

Autotype London

Mary Godsall del

PL. XVII

AUTOTYPE, LONDON.

PL. XVIII

PL XIX

MARY GODSALL DEL   AUTOTYPE, LONDON

PL. XX

AUTOTYPE, LONDON

PL. XXII

Autotype, London.

PL. XXIII

MARY GOOSALL DEL. AUTOTYPE, LONDON

PL. XXIV

AUTOTYPE. LONDON.

Pl. XXV

MARY GODSALL DEL.   AUTOTYPE, LONDON

PL. XXVII

AUTOTYPE, LONDON

PL. XXVIII

AUTOTYPE, LONDON.

MARY GODSALL DEL. ALTOT· PL. LONDON

PL. XXXI

PL. XXXIV

MARY GODSALL DEL. AUTOTYPE, LONDON.

PL. XXXV

Autotype, London.

PL. XXXVI

AUTOTYPE. LONDON.

PL. XXXVII

AUTOTYPE LONDON

PL. XXXVIII

AUTOTYPE, LONDON

PL. XLI

AUTOTYPE, LONDON

Pl. XLII

PL. XLIV

AUTOTYPE LONDON

PL. XIA

AUTOTYPE LONDON

PL. XLVII

AUTOTYPE, LONDON

Pl. XLVIII

AUTOTYPE, LONDON

Mary Goodsall del.   Antotype London

Pl. LI

MARY GOODSALL DEL.

AUTOTYPE, LONDON

 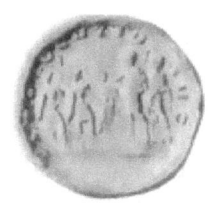

AUTOTYPE, LONDON

Pl. LIV

AUTOTYPE, LONDON

Pl. LV

Autotype, London

MARY GODSALL DEL. AUTOTYPE, LONDON

PL. LXI

AUTOTYPE. LONDON.

AUTOTYPE LONDON

www.ingramcontent.com/pod-product-compliance
Lightning Source LLC
Chambersburg PA
CBHW031339230426
43670CB00006B/378